Mary Cappello

TRANSIT
BOOKS

Published by Transit Books
2301 Telegraph Avenue, Oakland, California 94612
www.transitbooks.org

LIBRARY OF CONGRESS CATALOGING–IN–PUBLICATION DATA
Names: Cappello, Mary, author.
Title: Lecture / Mary Cappello.
Description: Oakland : Transit Books, 2020. | Series: Undelivered lectures
   | Includes bibliographical references.
Identifiers: LCCN 2020010036 (print) | LCCN 2020010037 (ebook) | ISBN
   9781945492426 (paperback) | ISBN 9781945492464 (ebook)
Subjects: LCSH: Lectures and lecturing. | Listening. | Public speaking.
Classification: LCC PN4193.L4 C37 2020 (print) | LCC PN4193.L4 (ebook) |
   DDC 808.5/1--dc23
LC record available at https://lccn.loc.gov/2020010036
LC ebook record available at https://lccn.loc.gov/2020010037

COVER DESIGN
Anna Morrison

TYPESETTING
Justin Carder

DISTRIBUTED BY
Consortium Book Sales & Distribution
(800) 283-3572 | cbsd.com

Printed in the United States of America

9 8 7 6 5 4 3 2 1

 This project is supported in part by an award from the National
Endowment for the Arts.

for Martin Leonard Pops (1934-2011)
and his lecturing art

"For what can be oppressive in our teaching is not, finally, the knowledge or the culture it conveys, but the discursive forms through which we propose them . . . And I am increasingly convinced, both in writing and in teaching, that the fundamental operation of this loosening method is, if one writes, fragmentation, and, if one teaches, digression, or, to put it in a preciously ambiguous word, excursion."

—Roland Barthes, "Lecture In Inauguration of the Chair of Literary Semiology, Collège de France, January 7, 1977"

"I used to think I wrote because there was something I wanted to say. Then I thought, 'I will continue to write because I have not yet said what I wanted to say'; but I know now I continue to write because I have not yet heard what I have been listening to."

—Mary Ruefle, *Madness, Rack and Honey: Collected Lectures*

I.

WHY

LECTURE?

In 1934, in curious approximation of a correspondence between Sigmund Freud and Albert Einstein, titled, "Why War?," Virginia Woolf published an essay with the cryptic title, "Why?" It was a call to bring the then over-abundance of lectures and lecturing to an end: if print media had replaced the lecture, why must we still attend lectures? "Why lecture, why be lectured?" At the heart of Woolf's essay lodges an unforgettable aphorism that goes: *Now the human voice is an instrument of varied power; it can enchant and it can soothe; it can rage and it can despair; but when it lectures it almost always bores.* Of course Woolf's essay, which quite possibly began as a lecture, does not bore. It is shot through with humor and novelistic *mise en scènes*; it is punctuated with fury and a series of ever-mounting repetitions that sound and resound into a magnificent rallying cry against the lecture and lecturing.

"*Why,*" Woolf asks, "continue an obsolete custom which not merely wastes time and temper, but incites the most debased of human passions—vanity, ostentation, self-assertion, and the desire to convert? Why encourage your elders to turn themselves into prigs and prophets, when they are ordinary men and women? Why force them to stand on a platform for forty minutes while you reflect upon the colour of their hair and the longevity of flies? Why not let them talk to you and listen to you, naturally and happily, on the floor? Why not create a new form of society founded on poverty and equality? Why not bring together people of all ages and both sexes and all shades of fame and obscurity so that they can talk, without mounting platforms or reading papers or wearing expensive clothes or eating expensive food? Would not such a society be worth, even as a form of education, all the papers on art and literature that have ever been read since the world began? . . . Why not invent human intercourse? Why not try?"

I am totally with Virginia Woolf in wanting to create a new form of colloquy, to move with others and across affiliations in the collective formation of ideas—to converse—to arrive at a dwelling in common where real discussion can be had; but, rather than ask "why lecture" with Woolf, I want to know if it is possible to re-inhabit what was great and stirring about the lecture when it was *a form of art*. This requires restoring the lecture's affiliation with the essay, not, in the process, to arrive at a lecture that comes to its point, and does so with dazzling aplomb, but to re-value wandering ways: to distinguish the boredom that lectures characteristically instill from the even-hovering attention they can incite; to court the counter-intuition of going on a journey with a wandering guide, then to share what is noticed—the marginal, the ephemeral—precisely because of the way that lecture holds you, as the necessary effect of its hover and drift.

Midway between a sermon and a bedtime story, the lecture is knowledge's dramatic form.

Nonfiction's lost performative: the lecture.

Cousin to the essay, or its precursor: that non-genre that allows for untoward movement, apposition, and assemblage, that is one part conundrum, one part accident, and that fosters a taste for discontinuity.

Now it's possible that no one who has been lectured to would wish to ponder this with me—the lecture as lost and forgotten literary form—because the "to" in the first place would have dispirited him. I mean, nothing about the poor lecturing habits most of us have fallen heir to would make us want to hang around and contemplate what had just happened from the vantage of our seat in the proverbial hall. "To" is just as bad as "at" where the lecture is concerned: in each case, you and I feature as a wall of sorts to which wet strands of spaghetti, once flung, might or might not stick. Moving in and around, behind and before, but never at; more circular than square, occasionally spiraling and looped, compressed and exhibited, exposing and exposed—that's the lecture I wish to contemplate of the still-to-be.

But why? As Woolf might ask. Why here? Why now?

In 2017 when I delivered the lecture from which this little book has grown, I found myself saying that as women we've still to take back the night, to say nothing of the lectern. We need to take back the lectern from Sean Spicer who uses the lectern as a prototype for his boss' wall, or as Melissa McCarthy instructs us, as a weapon: a literal bludgeon. "Don't lecture me!" Now lecture has a superannuated superego effect. When "lecture" becomes a homonym for "hector," we know we've fallen on bad times. I prefer "intone" as the lecture's operative verb—a lecture as an intonation on . . . an invitation toward . . . fill in the blank, fill in the verb.

Why turn our attention in the direction of the lecture? Because, no matter if we're writers or readers, students or teachers (and I'd venture to guess we're all always both, in or out of a classroom, in politics or in love), we want always to be rediscovering the forms that are at our disposal. To take nothing for granted. It's not enough to be conversant with the very modes by which the order of things is understood, conveyed, and shaped. We need actively to re-invent those. Following Michel Foucault, we want to "grasp the implicit systems which determine our most familiar behavior without our knowing it" [and thereby] "make the cultural unconscious apparent." To put into question our modes of enactment and conveyance, even to revolutionize them.

We want to create genealogies of forms that we tacitly endorse, and by which we come to know the world, or for that matter "learn" what we learn. Yes, what is at stake here is the relationship between nonfiction and pedagogy; between non-fiction and performance—*nonfiction off the page*; between non-fiction and information; and between nonfiction and perhaps most paramount of all—voice. Think of the great lecturers you have known if you've had the good fortune of knowing any. The essence of the lecture isn't the what but the how, how they say it, which is to say, inhabit it; embody it; sing it; or, to put this another way: is attendance at a lecture about a *will to knowledge* or *a will to listen*?

Mary Ruefle's wonderful *Madness, Rack and Honey*, subti-tled "Collected Lectures," is really a gathering of anti-lectures. There she writes of how her "innate horror of lectures" has to do with producing more language on language rather than in-volving herself in the creation of what Nemerov might call the silence of understanding to which all art aspires. She likens her recalcitrance around lecturing on poetry to the silence best kept around the thrush: "I do not think I really have anything to say about poetry other than remarking that it is a wandering little drift of unidentified sound, and trying to say more reminds me of following the sound of a thrush into the woods on a summer's eve—if you persist in following the thrush it will only recede deeper and deeper into the woods; you will never actually see the thrush . . . but I suppose listening is a kind of knowledge, or as close as one can come. 'Fret not after knowledge, I have none,' is what the thrush says. Perhaps we can use our knowledge to preserve a bit of space where his lack of knowledge can survive."

Is this collection of "untethered pieces" and "accumulated debris" in which subjects float by and never manifest into lectures, reflective, in the end, merely of Ruefle's ambivalence toward lectures, or does it find her mining that other form whose genealogy is also worth tracing: the note—the note as the origin of the lecture and the end toward which the lecture tends until, if we're lucky, we strike upon the note as pure form: aphorism. "A poem is a neutrino—mainly nothing—it has no mass and can pass through the earth undetected," is one of my favorites in this book. "Capitalism, like the Arctic environment, is a system THAT DOESN'T CARE IF YOU LIVE OR DIE," is another.

This is what her lecture delivers. Just bring these two aphorisms into a room and let them rub up against each other. Leave your books at home. Forget the lecture.

At least for now . . . but remember it later in a dream or in a note where it sounds unhesitatingly, reverberatingly. Whether a lecture unwinds across a long stretch of time (like this one), or is intent on condensation à la Ruefle, it makes me present to a new form of listening; it creates a new listener in me (like all great literature). The lecture as I want to imagine it is pedagogic without being didactic. The student it conjures doesn't work by way of a one to one correspondence as in a me here lecturing to a you there listening—listening for what is going to be on the test. The test will be your writing, the test will be your striking of a tuning fork, in harmony or in dissonance but never for or against, resonant and reverberant, nearby rather than opposed.

Even as I deliver this encomium to you (what the hell's an encomium?), I fear I don't know enough to lecture on it—to lecture on the lecture—but this is just a defense against what I know but don't dare say: that great lectures are irreducible to knowledge as such—they stir something in our souls that they ask us to heed. If they maintain the demeanor of a holy space, a temple even, this doesn't mean they are averse to bois-terousness or commotion; quite the contrary—a great lecture invites hubbub even as it clears a path to the sort of quietude where thought occurs. It does this without the aim of dogma or conversion. It argues without taking sides. It errs on the side of rapture rather than vehemence.

Your preference might be for a lecture that begins by put-ting the audience at ease rather than setting them on edge, and you are hopeful that this book will be peppered with anecdotes. But the lecture as I'm asking you to imagine it isn't stuffed with fun facts, so much as it is an organic matter-of-fact and just as compostable. At its best, it's all sparks and glimpses and this is what it leaves you with: a partial light that only barely wakes you and keeps you seeking more. If it wants something from us, it is this: desire wrapped in patience, a type of patience that can never know at what point a moment, hour, or day might break into atonality rather than lapse into narrative song.

The lecture, the lecture, the lecture—stay with me!—is a matter of privilege—everyone says so at the outset—"it's a great privilege to be here"—but rarely does the lecturer inter-rogate her privilege or the pillars that hold it in place. Think of the fumbling, bumbling or doddering lectures that mostly men are capable of, that so many of us have suffered through, and that give lectures a bad name—lectures, tight-lipped and assured they will be forgiven their wretchedness as they salute all the men in the room and the many more who are absent, who needn't woo you nor gain your interest because they don't really have you in mind. And there are other segregationist principles at work: the cordoning off of literary knowledge (writers speaking to writers—I'm culpable!), and academic research (scientists speaking to scientists)—with the "general public" and its elusive twin, "the general reader" left in the dust. Or the urge, on those rare occasions when she's allowed to ascend the podium, to turn away from a female body, young or aged, straight or queer, black or white, fat or thin, stupendously female and therefore likely to leave you to struggle with the barrage of epithets you need to suppress so powerful that you cough or wriggle or over-laugh.

For many of us, the lecture is the stuff of bad dreams, a sure locus of anxiety. If I'm a student in the nightmare, the lecture is the thing I'm impossibly late for or have missed; if I'm a teacher, it's that for which I am hopelessly unprepared. But what if the lecture were an opportunity for freedom; a conduit to a deeper place, a brighter consciousness rather than the medium for regulating what counts as knowledge, for measuring success or managing our failures? It's not what I say in a lecture but what it reminds you of or helps you to remember or tempts you to want to know that I hope you feel encouraged toward, and *that* relies on hints and whiffs, not information. In fact, subjugated knowledge is the thing I'm interested in. No matter the genre of art I am experiencing, that's usually where I want to be taken—to the left out and the leftover, to the forgotten or subordinated.

I say this, and yet I admit a nostalgic fondness for the thing that one must always say in a lecture, the phrase, "As we all know . . ." followed by a list of books and references that you know nothing about and after which you run out to find. Or, "As we will all remember . . ." It is an arrogant presumption, but, at the same time, I have to say I love the *share* of knowledge it tries to dream: the lecture as a rite of passage into a readership or a community or, well, I hope not, a club? Perhaps this is where the lecture fails, but if it makes us want to run to a library, (ok, or to the Internet), or run from it, or toward something we didn't know enough to want to run toward or away from before we heard it, that may be all to the good; if it tempts us to move differently, maybe that is all good.

In a 2013 interview for *Jezebel*, Anne Carson said, "I'm really trying to make people's minds move, you know, which is not something they're naturally inclined to do . . . We have a kind of inertia, sitting and listening. But it's really important to get somehow into the mind and make it move somewhere it has never moved before . . . Given whatever material we're going to talk about, and we all know what it is, how can we move within it in a way we've never moved before, mentally?"

As we will all remember, "the grove or garden in which the philosopher had walked back and forth as he spoke with the students was named the Lyceum, and the term was kept alive [during the Lyceum movement] by virtue of this association." Should I amble then? Should you do something other than sit still? Or is it that in essaying I rove in ways my body could not for trying? The movement that began in the U.S. in the late 1820s, according to Carl Bode's *The American Lyceum: Town Meeting of the Mind*, helped to shape a distinctive prose style in American Literature. (What would its analog be today? I'm not really aware of a distinctive prose style in America.) An institution through which lectures, dramatic performances, debates, and the like are presented to a community, the "main purpose of the movement originally was to provide practical scientific instruction for workmen, and to have as a result a more intelligent worker as well as a better product."

"Fully three quarters of Ralph Waldo Emerson's published writing began as lectures" that he delivered in the Lyceum. The lecture began to prove an essayistic ideal for him. We will remember the famous entry into Emerson's Journal, July 5, 1839: "A lecture is a new literature, which leaves aside all tradition, time, place, circumstance, and addresses an assembly as mere human beings, no more . . . it is an organ of sublime power, a panharmonicon for variety of note . . ." You don't need me to remind you who counted as human in 1839—the Emersons of that world and no one else. Yet I still want to give Emerson a modicum of credit for introducing a crack into the sexist, racist and classist façade of how we come to know things. Because the thing about Emerson was that he did not entertain his audiences, and in fact often irritated them; in other words, he eschewed complacency in public reception and public address. Moreover, though they often did not "understand what he said," they invited him back again and again.

Emerson's nineteenth century auditors must have had an appetite for atonality and disarray. They must have known something that is lost on us—like, that aphorisms are thorny and need more than a micro-brew to wash them down. The time of the lecture—like all that is beautiful about an essay's ruminative spell—is slow time. We could call it the time *of* understanding, over and against the time it takes *to* understand. Barthes calls it "a kind of divine time," a time that is "just" (as in fair, and laced with freedom), or, as he defines it—a "(delicate, slow, benevolent) passage from one logic to another, from one body to another." "If I had to create a god," he muses, "I would lend him a 'slow understanding'; a kind of drip-by-drip understanding of problems. People who understand quickly frighten me." Aphorisms slow us down, and don't wish to be consumed like advertising copy or slogans that tell us which way the wind blows and how to follow it. When twentieth century readers reduce Emerson's lectures to quotable quotes along the order of daily affirmations or *bon mots*, memorable one-liners, decked out in needlepoint or plastered onto calendars, they inadvertently negate that most famous one—"to be great is to be misunderstood," effectively neutralizing the dissonance at the heart of the lecture and the essay.

Did Emerson's nineteenth century audiences seek a language for the disconnect of their contemporary lives, something his lectures, would, at least, confirm? Dissonance in his comportment, in his voice, in his "message," and even especially in his sentences, rather than alienate people, seems to have kept them coming back. I like to think they were enticed by the hint of what they knew but dared not say: that a gulf loomed large between democracy on paper and in fact; that life as people lived it in the antebellum U.S. hardly met the requirements of democracy in principle and in act. Such disconnect is daily and insistent if you are alive to it, if you haven't shut it down or learned to medicate it, assuming you aren't privileged enough to ignore it. When you know what you know is *not* what you know but something else, unease is the result of the gap. The agreement to agree, the investment in a belief in a real all the while knowing that somehow, somewhere, you're *not* convinced, you *don't* believe in the ways your own reality has been structured; you don't believe in the real of the real of gender, of race, of fill in the blank, but you agree to pretend to. All great essays investigate the space between what one is told about the real and what one truly knows about it. This is the essay, and the lecture's, essential life-affirming disassociated ground, and our aim is to reconstitute it word by word, sentence by sentence, space by space.

What I wouldn't give for a glimpse at one of Emerson's audience member's notes. (Certainly they must have been given a Thoreauvian pencil at the door.) And now I'm remembering a sentence that might lie buried here, an effect of my enthusiasm and my having rushed it, like the girl in Henry James whose imagination jumps across several tracks while her foot is still lodged in the space between them. *The note is the origin of the lecture and the end toward which the lecture tends.* The lecture's fore and aft—the note. The lecture's tipping point, the note-book combines the energy of containment with the velocity of scatter. This is why its vitality cannot be underestimated as the lecture's wellspring and repository. It's the set of marks that prove you have found a way to remain inspired, against all odds, and it can't be reproduced; if it's stolen or lost, forgotten or misplaced, it cannot be replaced. Our notes are keys that await a hand to find the chord in them, the strangest sound inside an even stranger afternoon. They're a series of strategies, a record of arrangements, as beguiling as they are familiar. They're a pack of strays that cannot be corralled for all their mewling.

"Since I do not have all morning (your Dean asked me to limit myself to fifteen minutes at the utmost—'at the utmost' are his own words), I will say what I want to say without the step-by-step reasoning and the historical evidence to which you, as a gathering of students and scholars, are entitled."

—JM Coetzee, *Elizabeth Costello*

II.

LECTURE

MISCELLANY,

OR

STRAY CATS

A lecture can't be a celebrity sensation. It has to be experienced in the round. In place of the lecture hall, a mood room, the shape of whose atmosphere morphs to meet the contours of the subject-to-hand. At the entryway, participants can select from among a rotten tomato; a set of tiddlywinks; a cyanometer; a palette knife; a vomit bag; or a joint.

•

I once listened to a lecture that lasted three full hours and was not for a moment bored. It was an historian's assemblage of the vast networks of people who came and went through the doors of a villa in Central Europe that is now a meeting place for artists and intellectuals. He was supposed to create a pamphlet, but he got carried away. He carried us away. His commission was canceled.

•

When James Baldwin or Gilles Deleuze answer interview questions, it is not quite accurate to say that they reply "articulately"—it's not that they are eloquent merely—it's that they respond in essays, performative essays. Try mapping their moves and get a feel for the shape of their thought. Deleuze moves from preferences to self-effacement; propositions to questions; fascinations to definitions; self-questioning to neologisms all of which lay the ground for his arriving at a wild card as explanation for his original point of departure. Baldwin gives us prolonged parentheticals, emphatic turning points, gasps that give life to the gap between the Real as he knows it and racism's blaring falsehoods: list-like and conversational at once, his "answer" is a paean to a genre of knowledge one rarely finds in lectures—that which one must, of necessity, learn in order to Be. Each assertion is more and more truth-bound, more and more a proclamation of our shared ethical bearing in the world: "I know one thing from another"; "I know I was born, am gonna suffer, and am gonna die"; "I know that the only way to get through life is to know the worst things about it." "I know," he says, "that a person is more important than anything else. *Anything* else." And then he pauses before explaining to those who might not already know: "I've learned this because I've had to learn it."

•

The PechaKucha as contemporary innovative lecture claims to really condense the Power Point presentation, to insist on focus, but I think it confuses focus with speed.

•

Is the space between writing and lecturing that in the former we ask questions of ourselves (in private) and in the latter, we ask questions openly in public?

•

When Gertrude Stein set out to lecture in America, she tried to free herself altogether of a discourse of questions and of answers. We will recall her remarking in *Everybody's Autobiography*, "To me when a thing is really interesting is when there is no question and no answer; if there is then already the subject is not interesting."

•

When I gave readings from a book on "awkwardness," I used to build a performative silence into my opening remarks. When you do this, at first people think that you're having a break-down and act alarmed. The silence, which last a few beats, feels to the audience like an hour. What you are after, of course, is a break*through*—a jolt born of disarming quiet to cut through the static and the noise.

•

In a lecture, I compose myself and comport myself, but maybe it would be better if I incarnated myself as a bird and cooed from the rafters out of earshot and out of sight, inviting you to follow me into the silence.

•

In the lecture, speech meets writing rather than serve as its passive or inert delivery system.

•

During those same years in which Stein was doing her thing on the lecture circuit, there was a woman named Mary Brooks Adelsperger doing hers. "Adventures of a Modern Head Hunter" was the title of Adelsperger's larger than life lectures-in-sculpture, each of which represented a different human emotion. *Reason is a face whose contour is a reversed isosceles triangle. Credulity is represented by a grotesque white head covered with yellow hair. It has no eyes.* (Adelsperger was obviously prescient).

•

TECHNOCRACY

REASON

CONVENTIONALITY

THE LOUNGE LIZARD

Adventures
of
A Modern Head Hunter

MARY B. ADELSPERGER

Sculptor, Artist, Humorist   REDPATH BUREAU

In some disciplines, the lecture will always be accompanied by a plaque. When I read from my book *Swallow* in medical contexts, the physicians almost always gave me a plaque to commemorate the talk. My studio is filled with such slabs like so many headstones to a length of little deaths.

•

Richard Hamblyn in his *Invention of Clouds* describes "one of the great lost lectures"—it was the lecture that Constable was never able to materialize on the new science of meteorology before he died. Why would we want this lecture if we have his art?

•

To say that the lecture has no point is not to conclude it is pointless.

•

When I was a wisp of a girl, maybe 10 years old, my mother hailed a bus for us out of our working class suburb to attend a lecture by Margaret Mead in Center City Philadelphia. I don't recall a thing Mead said, but I was rapt by the staff she carried and how it propelled her to the stage like a holy crutch or divining rod. During this same era, and in this same room, we went to hear Allen Ginsberg give a reading. In lieu of a sampling of his poetry that day, he chanted OM for a full forty minutes.

•

David Antin's talk poetry is a type of poem-talk or poetry-as-lecture and it doesn't pay to try to read those on the page and hope to get the full effect.

•

"I dance, romp, howl, whimper, rage, lecture and spit on the page now." Siri Hustvedt closes an essay about coming into her own via psychoanalysis with that line.

•

Erving Goffman in his wonderful "Lecture on the Lecture" (1977) meditates on the aspects of a lecture that cannot translate into printed prose, reminding us, "As a source of potential noise, the podium itself is a many-layered thing. One source we owe to the fact that lecturers come equipped with bodies, and bodies can easily introduce visual and audio effects unconnected with the speech stream, and these may be distracting. A speaker must breathe, fidget a little, scratch occasionally, and may feel cause to cough, brush back his hair, straighten her skirt, sniffle, take a drink of water, finger her pearls, clean his glasses, burp, shift from one foot to another, sway, manneristically, button and unbutton a jacket, turn the pages and square them off, and so forth—not to mention tripping over the carpet or appearing not to be entirely zipped up."

•

Is corporeality the essence of the lecture or its enemy? Is the real lecture to be found in the lecturer's bodily marginalia—all

that escapes the lecture even as it pleads for attempt at access—
or in her words?

•

I will never forget the first time I was moved to tears by a lecture:
it was that of Susan Howe on Emily Dickinson's fascicles circa
1986. Imagine being present to Audre Lorde as she addressed
the Modern Language Association in 1977. What a different Association that must have been then, I mean, has there ever been
a more significant lecture in those precincts before or since? And
with it, the seeds to her future prose, inspired, in part, she said,
when she heard Barbara Smith at a plenary session at that same
convention in the previous year stand up and identify herself as
a black lesbian literary critic wondering if she could actually "be
a black lesbian writer and live to tell about it."

•

I wish I had been alive to attend the lecture halls of France
in May '68; or how about the shadowy nooks and hushed
hubbub of the halls that bedeck great modernist novels? *The
Bostonians* or *Howard's End*? Nobody really "does" the lecture
in novelistic prose as well as Henry James does. Take his description of Verena Tarrant as she lectures from the point of
view of the stalker-suitor, Basil Ransom, who would wish to

silence her: "She moved freely in her exposed isolation, yet with great sobriety of gesture; there was no table in front of her, and she had no notes in her hand, but stood there like an actress before the footlights, or a singer spinning vocal sounds to a silver thread. There was such a risk that a slim provincial girl, pretending to fascinate a couple hundred blasé New Yorkers by simply giving them her ideas, would fail of her effect, that at the end of a few moments Basil Ransom became aware that he was watching her in very much the same excited way as if she had been performing, high above his head, on the trapeze. Yet as one listened, it was impossible not to perceive that she was in perfect possession of her faculties, her subject, her audience . . ."

•

TED Talks give me the creeps. Please do not confuse them with lectures. They all have a whiff of organized religion about them and the feel of the sermon on the infomercial mount.

•

Lecture: one person is required to think on her feet while all others are expected to think in their seat.

•

Imagine a book made of everyone's unasked questions at lectures, and the various reasons for WHY you never asked them: because cordiality must be maintained and your particular question might sound unkind; because "our format tonight does not allow for questions"; because when you tried to ask, your neck stuck in place, and your heart rose to lodge in your throat; because the truest sign of the visiting writer's accomplishments was that she reserved the right *not* to take questions; because when I say, "Did I answer your question?," you know it means I did not and you shall not press it; because it's an unspoken rule that the question, "Are there any questions?" means "It's ok to stop thinking now. Will you please shut up."

•

The lecture will have succeeded, if, like the essay, it cannot be summarized, but only experienced. Its geography is a theater-cocoon, descended from the study carrel where you read, the dark corner of the library you retreated into, which was descended from the cubbyhole you stowed your books and drawings in in kindergarten. But this is my sedimentation, not yours, and perhaps the experience of reading in the digital age does not conjure this at all.

•

The true scholar has an inexplicable staying power and is therefore likely to be the one least likely to leave before the close of the lecture. He enjoys the necessity of getting lost in the shape of someone else's lostness.

•

There are many ways in which a lecture can be interrupted— by polar bears (see my friend Russell Potter's experiences in lecturing on Arctic Cruises); by mass shootings (see classrooms in the United States of America); or by women (see Wittgenstein, who apparently would stop lecturing if a woman was in the room, only to resume after she left). I've no intention of trivializing violence by bracing it with polar bears and women; quite the contrary, I want my examples to point up the ways in which just as women (often enough the targeted victims in lecture halls) and polar bears (under threat of mass extinction) are casualties of a white male death-drive they play no part in, so the lecture, as paean to altruism, subtlety, and grace is always under threat of being vanquished in an instant by the intrusion of the spectacular violence it also seeks to thwart.

•

Beware occasions that entail too many administrative preludes to a lecture rendered in bureaucratese, as if to say, if the lecturer is worth his salt, he must also be worth this endlessly time-wasting wait. At times like these, recall instead those many occasions on which someone you revere—usually an unsung poet in a library with no more than ten filled chairs—is *left to introduce themselves*, and how they aren't expecting this and they are expecting this, and how they bring their son to play guitar in softly interpretive accompaniment of what is read, and how the audience speaks afterwards of the rare and calming atmosphere the entire event achieves.

·

Sometimes the names that populate a lecture drop like a pelting rain; sometimes they arrive as a soft mist or none too transparent cloak that, by dotting the page with the proper filiations, makes the speaker a temporary father of the pack. Sometimes they stride across the room in the form of a dutiful trot like the recitation of our age, ranks, and serial numbers; other times, and relatedly, they appear to placate the imagined gaze of the figure who looks over our shoulder, or whose breath is increasingly heavy on our necks. Rarely do I invoke the name of my great-grandmother (as Giuseppina Conte once said), or the local tailor (as Mike DiFabio was wont to ask), or my four year old niece (as Ava Cappello quipped the other day) even though who I talk to is as constitutive of my thinking as who I read and more likely to infuse the lecture with uncommon insight, or mark the stage on which we perform our share of knowledge as a quotidian ground.

•

What if the lecture began with questions from the audience and moved out from there? To dispense with the hierarchy of introductions (that no one listens to), words of thanks (ditto), easing in and inviting you (you continue not to listen), and go directly to the Q and A. Start there. But instead of your Q to my A, you give me an A for which I supply an A to which you supply a Q with A to which I supply an AQQA and so on until a tempo of thought emerges.

•

Each of us in our lifetimes should get to experience at least one life-changing lecture. For Whitman, we will recall, it was Emerson's "The Poet," delivered at The New York Societal Library in Manhattan on March 5, 1842. "I was simmering, simmering, simmering," Whitman wrote, "Emerson brought me to a boil." And, "the lecture was one of the richest and most beautiful compositions, both for its matter and style, we have heard anywhere at any time." For Hazlitt, it was hearing Coleridge, after which the landscape stopped being itself. For Sir Arthur Quiller-Couch (aka "Q"), the English literary critic responsible for that best of all writerly advice—"kill all your darlings"—it was "the thrill . . . of listening to Ruskin—cadaverous, his voice attenuated as a ghost's, his reason trembling at the last. But there was the man, and he was speaking . . ." For my friend Desirae Matherly, author of *Echo's Fugue*, it was Stravinsky's *Poetics of Music*, of course, but also Michael Faraday's *Chemical History of a Candle* introduced to her by Mary Ruefle. Desirae didn't need to be present in their day and age; she read their lectures and then composed imagined conversations with them. Perhaps all great lectures lead back to Mary Ruefle.

•

All novels begin as notes taken at imaginary lectures, some terrible, some great.

•

Here's a list of notable essayist-lecturers—though none would call themselves that—in the Age of Trump, each, in their way inventors of the forms they inhabit, and who overturn and displace, for me, the reality TV show writ large the Oval Officer has staged in the form of our newsfeeds. Sandra Bernhard (*Sandemonium*); Anna Deavere Smith (*Notes from the Field*); Christian Marclay (*The Clock*); Randy Rainbow ("There Is Nothin' Like a Wall"); Tracie Morris ("Slave Sho to Video aka Black but Beautiful" and "Little Girl").

•

If the sexist philosopher hordes his lecture-knowledge, it must be because he senses but fails to fully understand that knowledge bodies forth and spatializes just as ideation builds and breathes, pierces and subtends, stirs, rouses, filters, flies, unloosens, sings.

•

To lecture in the guise of the female body is always to risk attack, at best, and at worst, incomprehension—because we still have no way to figure intelligence in a female form, no way to picture a combination of startling truth and un-gendered beauty. I if I find my body quaking behind the podium it's because I'm excited to be messing with your minds, but also because I know you want to shoot me (down). It is for this reason that my lecture mustn't be aimed at resisting attack in the battle I've already lost from the outset; it mustn't defend or argue but catch you unawares; it must pinch you while you're sleeping, or better yet, lull you to sleep while asking you to climb its operatic steeps, sans pacifier; to lay down your arms and prick up your ears enough to tune in to its breathing.

•

It's the nature of a lecture never to be temporally adequate to its subject—that's the challenge of its constraint, and what makes it a perfect desiring machine: because the lecture always will fall short on time, it reserves the right to go on and on and on.

•

More and more, I have come to understand that the lecture wants nothing so much as to touch us; to instruct us in the power inherent in looking kindly on thought. If I could learn to look kindly on thought, I might come to look more kindly at—to hear with more compassion—the stuff that my own mind produces that I fail to understand. The lecture embraces—it has learned to love ideas. At best, it listens, and looks out for, a voice intent on singing, no longer cowed before the bully pulpit of the mind.

I'm remembering the time I suggested we play the "lecture" game with the eight- and nine-year-old children of my friends. We pretended each to give a lecture on the subject of "nothing." We used the word "indubitably" a lot; we put on airs; we donned regalia; we tapped on our students' heads during the Q and A; we broached a great deal of nonsense and we had a lot of fun.

The zero is the nothing of the no-time and if we WERE to consider this ahem as in the hem that is missing all about your skirt thus is absence this is indeed the preview of the non-matter that is the none-sense of no-THING pings and all this nottingale and ahem ahem ARE you listening I fear you have MISSSED the point quite rightly or wrongly and there-there yes hold your horses young man I'll call on you in time but first some words on the goose egg of minus-1 before but never aft open but not closed after all at the beginning and at the end this is the garble of the garbage that I chomp and nothing more quoth the raven never is anything like nothing or is it not?

We played like this, the kids and I, basically saying whatever came to mind on "nothing" until we were overcome with belly laughs, and what came to the fore as we played The Lecture Game was how the kids already knew what "smart" sounds like and how to imitate it by way of emphasis but also how, by putting the authority of the lecture in quotation marks, we were able to experience free associative fun rather than the need to "get things right," to "know one's stuff." The lecture as liberatory.

"What is the origin of the podium?" a hand shoots up—and I an-swer, "Poppycock or postulate, propagate or pollinate, dopamine and punctuate: thus we arrive at the origin of the "podium" at which I stand. The podium's origin is, and is not, obvious. The (obviously Greek) word 'podium' derives from the temple-like enclosures in which elders placed themselves intent to receive the idioms of the gods (note the crucial homonym—pod/god,) and the angle at which one set the mystic writing pad—a palimpsest really—was just as crucial. In fact

the first podiums deliver to us our sense of the word "angle" understood as vantage or position, said angle being dependent upon the lecturer's intuition for aligning the template (see, earlier, temple) properly or in tune with the Euclidean disposition of that day's arrangement of heavenly stars. Our inheritance of the rostrum (but that word is for a different day) has of course lost all of this meaning: now the podium simply serves as a prop since all divine intermediaries abandoned we humans long ago. Thus we find in the podium one of numerous forms whose original meaning is lost to us but that we still rely upon to, well, prop us up, its angle now a mere expediency for reflecting the light properly upon the page and reducing neck strain. I for one will always request a podium to shield my shaking body from view. (The disembodiment of the lecturer, you will note, allows us to retain the presence of a god but not one on whom we can in the least rely. It is in this sense that a podium remains essential to the lecturer: for, even while it is true that we can do no better than teeter on the precipice of non-knowledge, that we are perforce beholden to a metaphysics of float, drift and drown, we find it necessary to retain the illusion that it is firm ground from which we speak. Otherwise, who would listen to us?)

Lectures such as these need no auspices or guarantors, no contract or occasion save for our meeting face to face in a room set off to the side, a lost play's lean-to.

Look, there's something serious going on here . . .

    When I was a young writer, having just turned eighteen, I pictured myself literally as a man when I visualized giving voice to my poetry in public. As though when I tried to dream myself into a writer-in-public, or to fantasize, a male dummy entered where my voice and body should have been. Thirty years later at the verdant epicenter of a small amphitheater in Palazzolo Acreide, Sicily, I felt I'd found my place, the spirit welling within me and the words sprouting from foot through crown in vowels that could stir as much as quiet, even though I knew, in its (ancient Greek or Roman) day, no woman would be wanted there except as figure or idea.

Could my voice fill an amphitheater, or my body? Can yours?

Etymologically: lecturer means "reader"; he who reads to.

Were the earliest lectures intended to educate those who did not yet know how to read, or who had no time for it; to instruct an audience in reading; or to create an envelope of otherness in which a collective imagination could congregate for a time? Probably none of the above, pre-printing press; but even if the lecture was merely an expedient way to transmit a text to a scribe, there had to be something ennobling and humbling, arduous and committed, principled and concentrated and embodied about the enterprise. I'm just not sure of "playful." I only know that what gets displaced by the graying term—"lecture"—is not only its multifarious origins and locales, the nascent beauty of a unique address, but the forms of noticing it has the potential to invite its audience to experiment with as respondent. Isn't it obvious that we'd arrive at a different species of understanding if, instead of recording data points, we were asked to note what the lecture reminds us of, what it prompts us to remember, and what it makes us want to know? But these are my questions born of an essayistic interest in that migratory movement Cynthia Ozick once described that finds an essay moving "from reality to memory to dreamscape and back again." My questions are meant to invite a companion consciousness into the lecture hall, then to see what we make from it all in the form of our notebooks. The threadbare pages that we tread, less with worry than with want, I call our "notes." Fastened to our seats in the lecture hall, we aren't funnel-heads into which a lecturer's knowledge is poured. We are haunted beings trailed by past trials, we are shadows of our barely realized truths, evidence of our existence, bathed in the light, or dark, of future wanderings. Our notebooks are a signature snow globe whose flecks are the things we remember, floating inside the things we've yet to glimpse. Even an occasional shake can tempt our lives toward something more than a dim assemblage of rote transactions and the automated reaching toward a cellphone.

Let's begin by forging something from a stray mark upon the page.

Let's draw a picture of what we think is least important.

Let us open our notebooks and start from scratch.

III.

TAKE

NOTE

"The room to begin with had a hybrid look—it was not for sitting in, nor yet for eating in. Perhaps there was a map on the wall; certainly there was a table on a platform, and several rows of rather small, rather hard, comfortless little chairs. These were occupied intermittently, as if they shunned each other's company, by people of both sexes, and some had notebooks and were tapping their fountain pens, and some had none and gazed with the vacancy and placidity of bullfrogs at the ceiling."

—Virginia Woolf, "Why?"

SECTION ONE: SCAFFOLD

Let us begin again, (as though nothing has of yet been said), by reading a passage from Louise Bogan's journals as she attempted to write a lecture on women poets for Bennington College in September 1962:

> *5 September*
> *I am at last covering paper, in the matter of the women's poetry piece, and I bought a red pencil, yesterday, with which to make loops . . .*

> *8 September*
> *I am surrounded by pine-needles, mushrooms, and lovely late flowers. The actual writing of the piece will begin on Monday.*

> *18 September*
> *The piece is slowly getting into form—quite different than originally planned.*

19 September
Only three or four full days of work left. The piece is advancing, but it keeps changing under the pen. V. strange. I may end up with just a bunch of detached sentences.

3 October
The piece is being copied out on the typewriter; It looks very different than I thought. I hope to have it all on blue paper by Friday, and rewrite over the weekend.

9 October
My piece is in the 2nd typescript stage, and seems rather imbecilic, at present. V. light in tone . . . If they don't laugh during the first five minutes, I'll just start cutting, as I go along.

Eventually she arrives at the opening lines of the actual lecture as follows:

11 October
It is sometimes a good thing—a fortunate development—when a piece of writing turns out to be quite different from what its author originally planned. Change of direction, even after a paper is well started, is, at best, a sign that the facts involved—and the writer's feeling about the facts—are fairly lively; are not merely a series of clichés or a file of dead notions. They move and breathe, and given their head, often combine and re-combine in interesting and unexpected ways.

I feel envious of Bogan for her only having taken a month to compose her lecture since it feels, where this one is concerned, I've been writing it my whole life, and have yet to get it properly down on paper. But all that teaches me is the devotional nature sans solemnity described here in her notebook, because I know nothing that requires more faith or dedication than writing, more patience and more hopefulness than sitting in a lecture hall listening to someone read to you. Like an essayist, the lecturer will only lose the interest at the center of this thing called "thought" whose movement lives inside us if she insists from the outset on knowing what she will address, how she will conclude and by what means say it. Consequently, the lecture craves the traces of how its auditors think *with* rather than *of* it, new turns of thought that "combine and recombine," and that can only be found in your notes.

Glory be to god for our notebooks and the way the notebook builds like the making of a nest or a quilt (see pine needles) so that you will never have to shiver in the otherwise cold lecture hall no matter how barren a thought or word or tenor, and I feel sorry for my students who never learned the art and joy and necessity of noting—how it becomes a reserve and a refuge and a place of requisite making, crowded with mysteries and short-hands that are always poignant for the way they remind us of the essential untranslatability of ourselves to ourselves and especially of ourselves to others, and how tentative language is at the same time that it is all that we have.

The kind of noting I have in mind thwarts authority; it

scribbles and doodles and parries; it is so much ejecta bleeding between the lines and nothing can subdue its liveliness even when it is jotted under cover of loll. It doesn't stand at attention like bullet points and may not even need ruled paper but treats the page as a field of play as individual as our bodies and as unique as the means at our disposal for having conversations with ourselves; with the dead; or with some future art(ist) whose hands for once shall not be tied.

Here's a notebook of plush proportions, and another of scattered bits. *The Golden Notebook. The Notebooks of Malte Laurids Brigge. Notes of a Native Son. The Prison Notebooks. Notes on Camp.* Books by philosophers were often enough compilations of notes taken by their students during lectures—see, for example, Simone Weil's *Lectures on Philosophy*, a collection of lecture notes taken by one of her students during the academic year 1933-34. There is a place, even a need, for notes, I guess, that attempt to be "faithful" to the lecture, or transcriptive. But then there is a book comprised of the notes upon which a lecturer based his lectures: I'm thinking of Barthes' off-the-beaten path, *The Neutral*, the idiosyncrasy of whose signature traces may be illegible even to the lecturer himself but that nevertheless yields a *matter of mind* that is often lost when the notes are translated into an integrated, narrative whole. It seems obvious that to write is to apply a steadying device to the dizzying effects of our notebooks' vortices, but it seems equally true that the great writer finds a way to retain the notebook's signature plumb-line and design, however cock-eyed, rather than wipe the shape of its meanderings clean or denude it of its grace. Our notes are no doubt of a similar order as that private hieroglyphic (no psychologist has ever studied) by which we come to highlight points upon the pages of a book we are reading: you use vertical lines in rows of one, two, or three; brackets; and squiggles. I use asterisks, dots, arrowheads; I underline some things with a straight or wavy line (there is a difference), draw boxes around others, and at other times cradle the start of a sentence with a half-moon. Once, on opening a used copy of a book I had purchased, I found myself surprised to see that a previous reader had crossed out entire sentences, and in some cases, paragraphs of the writer's prose. But when I looked more closely, I realized that their mark wasn't intended as an erasure but as a highlighter: they had illuminated sentences they experienced as key by rubbing them lightly with the side of a pencil, first in one direction, then in the other. The effect was to create a crosshatch that made the letters they had marked stand out. This reader must have been an artist. Everything is telling.

What's sad to see is how yesterday's notebook is today's self-management attaché: in a world comprised of the most complex data storage systems ever devised, we're reverting with a desperate urgency to the material notebook in the form of the "bullet journal" and its attendant industry of guidebooks and videos and even crash courses in how to make one. Someone offered to convert me once, and being susceptible, I almost bit. She showed me her life arrayed in boxes, ready to be filled or otherwise "accomplished." Though these books are clearly aimed at calming our shared chaos, antidotes to the *glut* our computers claim to store, their extraordinary spread of colored markers reveals nothing so much as the darkest dystopia outlined in black and colored in rainbow.

Open your notebook and discover a personal map of the terra incognita of your soul, which isn't to say that our souls are without influence. Lectures are utterances; books are articulations; notes are marks, but that doesn't mean they're voiceless.

In my case, I'm sure that my note-taking tendencies were influenced by those of my mother's father's journals. He was a self-described "obscure cobbler" who jotted his writing onto the materials of his shoe-making trade, whole treatises squeezed onto the back of the tab used to mark down what part of the shoe needed fixing, with a word inevitably broken by the hole-punched "O" at the top or the bottom of the tab. Some pieces—mounds of odd-sized paper bits with writing on them, philosophical, urbane, poetic, reverential as daily prayers—he collected into shoe boxes labeled: 'Fragments of erratic thoughts from Llans Cobbler.' (His real name was John Petracca). To muse, to speculate, to wonder, to see: these are the infinitives he allowed to punctuate his work day, leaving me with tantalizing collage-texts that ask me to intuit their dream-shape of look, rest, chart, and turn. I described their enigma in my very first book, *Night Bloom*, over twenty years ago, only understanding years later how they served most intimately as its base. On one sheet he braces a neatly scribed list of the day's doings with ardent observations and subtly parsed conundrums. Everything is notable, the seemingly significant and the seemingly insignificant are worthy of a shared page, but each is also carefully lent a different sort of hand. Thematically, they range across several wars and three recurrent themes: his desire to be a writer in a language that would shun him; the beauty and importance of artisanal work, the plying of a trade; and his attempt to understand the politics of his poverty, convinced of the power of humility, distinct from acceptance of or resignation to his plight.

In the early 1960s, when he worked for less than minimum wage sorting mail in the basement of a major American banking complex, he also appears to have sorted his thoughts onto pages folded neatly into a pocket or a lunch box. These notes' dispositions seem literally to materialize one of his homespun maxims: "I must look at life upside down if I want to see my ideas come true!" Rather than record each new entry to conform to a predetermined left to right, top to bottom line, he shifted the line each day by turning the page to a different angle before he began to write. Each entry, I sometimes think, appears like a smaller or larger number on the clock face of the page, and I am compelled therefore, to read the passages in a clockwise manner, turning the page, like a wheel of time, as I go. Some put me in mind of pinwheels, flower centers with petals, splayed; or is this more like roulette? Are his note pages one part whimsy and two parts fate? Their moves between large looking-glass fonts to micro-scripts can leave a reader unsure about whether she should crane to know what some words say or simply experience them for their visual aspect. Take two miniature "pieces" of writing that flash like mini-beacons inside a field of blue and white. I assume that the words etched into these tiny rhymed columns must be significant because they seem to have been placed just so. I have to squint to read: "Five minutes of rest I am having to let my body relax so I can resume my work," and "2 pm I can see hailing, snowing and little rain." At first the words are almost disappointing in the seeming insignificance of what they record. On second take,

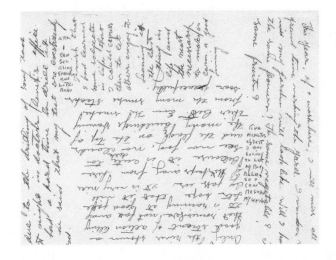

I experience them as the redolent pauses, the breaths in my grandfather's workday, a form of sacred time, infinitesimally small and full of life. That's the metaphysic, but the physic tells a different truth, the shape of poverty. Each entry is written at a different angle so that it will take up less room, so that my grandfather may conserve paper. At various times, he remarks—a condition beyond my ken—how he cannot afford to buy a writing tablet. Whether the words actually take up less space in their collage configuration than they would if he followed a standard linear format is neither here nor there; what is important is that the angle of his entries gives the illusion of space, it makes the page seem bigger than it is. But this is an abstract reading, to be sure; what's nearly impossible to read is the way the page brims with the intimate nature of one person's thoughts or one person's work day: all that "surrounds" the columns, in other words, from forms of self-soothing, to self-accusation, to assertions of the right and need to dream. The short passages contain so much—everything from the fear of losing a tooth—"I don't mind the pain only the thought of losing another tooth that has been so good to me for so many years. It is bitter. Losing good friends is never fun"—to descriptions of the weather (gentle fog); from dismay around how this work will take him from his garden—"This year of work here, I will miss all my grand time working in the yard.

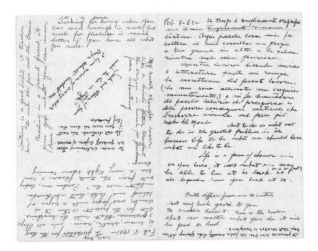

I wonder what my garden will look like. Will I have the same flowers? The same vegetables? The same fruits?" to his sense of having missed a formal education—"I wish that I had learned some subjects in life that I could express them to let others enjoy it." One passage, on this same page, in Italian, conveys a desire to read, in the five minutes allotted him, "infinite letters," driving home, again, how any notebook page is, at the least, a route to an opening, in time, in space, a trace of our existence within it.

Italians are known for being able to make gardens out of the smallest, driest patches of earth. Conservation, condensation, consolidation, if they are to retain the expansiveness and infinitude of a person's spirit, require toil, concentration, patience, and care. Throughout his life, my grandfather gave the most space to the sparest form, and here the lecture returns, once more, to aphorism: home-spun maxims, one-line poems, are one of his greatest pleasures. "The good old man standing on the corner of 4th and Chestnut selling pretzels shabby but alert faces the elements without fear nor protest"/"honesty is a lane full of thorns but it ends at the temple of love and peace"/ "work and starve if you want to be in style"/"on the same pedestal for the simple worker stands the unlegalized and legalized protection"/"shame it is that hatred is the fruit of poverty," and one that, though I will never know the full meaning of, I can sort of guess: "the articolist is a man of knowledge but his statements are very much controlled by the protection brain."

Is the "articolist" derived from Italian "articolare," to articulate, in which case, is the articolist a lecturer, and how can we shake loose of the "protection brain"? In Italian, it turns out, an "articolista" is a columnist, so this might be a commentary on journalism and a veiled argument for aphorism as the form most likely to upend the journalistic "statements" of his day.

Let me offer some of my own notes as exhibits A through E, all taken *in situ* in rooms and auditoria small, large, abutted by courtyards and windows, or boxed in, most occurring at the university where I teach save for a film screening in a cabin in Maine: I present you with these notes taken at one of the most gorgeous lectures I have ever had the good fortune to be present to, Martha Werner's "Weathering: Reading the Snell Family Meteorological Journal in the Long Days of the

Anthropocene"; notes taken during Masha Gessen's talk on *The Future is History* (my handwriting here is least legible of all as I was overcome with the electricity of their genius); notes taken while screening the Brother Quay's new film, based on a story by Uruguayan fabulist Felisberto Hernández, "The Balcony" (ditto); notes taken at a discussion by jazz trumpeter Paul Brody of the Semer Project to recover Jewish music and musicians who perished in the Holocaust; notes taken at a lecture titled, "Italy Calls Africa: Rhymes and Images Across

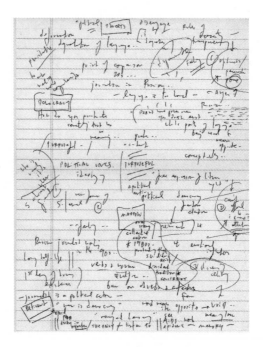

the Mediterranean" delivered by Allessandra DiMaio from the University of Palermo. Much less artfully articulated than my grandfather's journals, my lecture-based notebook pages seem like virtual landscapes in which the smallest speck and brightest shrub co-populate and mutually murmur at the same time that they are caught up in a subtle competition for emphasis. The loose leaved surface seems to want to expand into three and four dimensions when it only has two; it doesn't offer a *list* of highlights, though it does seem intent on creating a *cosmology*

with the page as firmament and "points" as planets transmitted by a lecturer's words and tones (dare I say, "vibrations"?) as they strike the ear and hand. If our individual notebook pages present an unsuspecting reader with a veritable "mess," that's significant—it reminds us of what's beautiful about anybody's notebook page, the notebook page as an index of disruptions into the listener's usually reliable concentrating mechanisms.

Across the realms of different discourses these lectures explore, I find some lines in common, a hidden poem on the nature of injustice and a world falling into the sea:

when does an image feel blank? // software to reconstruct the shredded Stasi documents // artifact as a spur to thinking // its mysterious waters and the assumption of a boat// to be enclosed by the Open// TUNA—local people do not want to eat because of thought of fish feeding on corpses (of refugees) // "The Declaration of Human Rights" // degradation of language—perishable—dispassionate // the hermetic form

"Edmund [Wilson] speaks of Emerson's lack of real intellectual power: the essays are flashes, held together by no structure of 'fundamental brainwork.' And the thought struck me that I should take notes happily all my life, not ever troubling to put them into form."

—Louise Bogan, *Journey Around My Room*

SECTION TWO: SUBDIVISION

When I think of books or works I love that reference the "note" in their titles, I begin to realize that it's not the note as such that is the defining feature of these books, but the preposition that accompanies the word: *Notes OF a Native Son; Notes ON Camp; Notes FROM Underground*. In the first case, the weight falls on the particular subject position of the writer. What makes the note signify is the "Native Son," James Baldwin, whose notes these are. In the second case, the phrase deflects our attention away from polemic even though the essay overflows with assertions. There is a certain authorial insouciance that becomes possible when I deign to publish my "notes on" anything, as if to say one can only claim such indefinite a phrase for a title if one is feeling very definite about oneself. But, then, to combine the "note" with "camp" is to ironize the note itself, decked out as an Oscar Wildean aphorism, and Sontag's "notes on," in this case, is more audacious than strictly philosophic. In the case of the marvelous Dostoevsky title (and I have to say I don't know how it sounds in the original Russian), the place from which the notes issue takes top billing, and this requires that we heed the type of notes these are (like those secreted in a bottle or furtively slipped through the chink in a wall); their intended recipient (surely not me, not you, but some accidental or imagined Other); and the ambiguity of their authorship (are they those we'd rather suppress, sent from unconscious to conscious? those scripted in a hand not our own but issuing through us? those that will tarnish the minute they hit the light of day or the piercing eye of the wrong recipient?)

Notes are never neutral.

Take the "extreme literary empiricism" of Georges Perec's post–Holocaust, post–May '68, *An Attempt at Exhausting a Place in Paris* (translated by Marc Lowenthal) alongside Dziga Vertov's post–Bolshevik Revolution manifesti on the camera eye as exceptionally attentive note-taker. Both projects are underscored by a distinctive *politics* of noting, in the first instance of the "infraordinary," or as Lowenthal describes it, "the humdrum, the nonevent, the everyday—'what happens,' as [Perec] puts it, 'when nothing happens other than the weather, people, cars, and clouds,'" and in the second instance, of what Vertov calls "life caught unawares." The constraint that Perec gave to himself was to return to the same Parisian locale over the course of three days, and to record "that which is generally not taken note of, that which is not noticed, that which has no importance." A fastidiously observed record of quotidiana, the book erupts into a subtly divined poetry of all that slips past the surveying gaze of the omnipresent police.

Perec is always working within and against the de-realization of the Holocaust and its diabolic inventories. In this, I am re-minded of Osip Mandelstam and how those few who survived him—(at least 1500 writers died under Stalinism between 1924 and 1953)—held fast to the belief that someone had scrawled onto a labor camp wall a line from one of his poems, even though it was never clear where and when exactly Mandelstam died. That sentence read: "Am I real and will death really come?" Like Vertov working in a much earlier period, Perec's hyper-realism is never hard-edged—it matches atrocity with ebullience, playfulness, and even laughter. For a politics of noting, there was none better than Vertov, whose dedication to visual phenomena only accessible to the camera eye, had as its self-expressed aim "so that we not forget what happens and what the future must take into account."

We come into the world handled, carried, and it is hoped, caressed, passed from hand to hand to hand, and gaze to gaze, a life-giving relay that yields in time a painstaking and laborious self-configuration arrived at via endless forms of representation, all of them historically grounded and politically imbued; we learn, if you will, to see, and by extension, to know, think and feel. Imagine having the audacity to try to alter characteristic modes of perception and discourse by way of your notational art, as Perec, as Vertov, did, convinced that this is where political change begins.

Imagine how this requires that we do some noting about noting, that we study our relationship to how and what we note. To do that, let's put to one side all the things we know about notes—for example, that they range in registers of mere mention to emphases, from enumerations to underscores—then climb a winding stair of counter-intuitions, like:

- that notes are the minima that constitute a life

- that in the notebook everything is plagiarized and nothing is

- that a note will never tell us if it aims to finish a thought or begin one, only that it wishes neither to complete nor conclude

- that some notes are nothing more than desperate attempts to "latch" on (here, Melanie Klein has a field day)

- that the writer is the person on whom nothing is lost but who also, in order to write anything, needs to act on what's important, i.e., to choose

- that the note is a diminutive genre or minor literature—I mean, would anyone's claim to fame be that they were an accomplished notetaker? That they had created in the little lives we're given not the consummate book or film or painting, but the consummate note? This is a good thing—too much pressure would kill the note and keep it from holding thought in suspension; plus, ask any essayist you know and they are always more happy to be listed as a "notable" essayist, and thus an essayist of interest, than be marred by the finality of a "best"

• that though we consider the note the most natural recording device, it is hard to know whether we note to remember or note to forget

• that to transcribe is just that—to bring a message across a threshold

• that noteworthy is redundant

• that the problem with the books that we write is that they are written in one language and one language only whereas our notes in every case represent a congregation of different types of signs and are rarely univocal

• that foot-, end-, and liner-notes each are different types of steps on an Escher-esque ladder of knowing

• that, in our current age, the worst form of noting is the trash genre, typically anonymous, called the "comment"

• that there is possibly no note that doesn't position the

writer as amanuensis, requiring therefore a master text, out of view, that the notebook serves. I have found no way to get around this.

- that if the notecard is the book's filing system and therefore also its kernel or code, we might try translating it backwards to see where it arrives rather than forward into fast-moving paragraphs of prose

- that there are those who will consider this so much silliness—the notebook as impenetrable abstraction, often unreadable even by oneself—and others who will recognize it as the workshop of our appetites and our strivings, the oft-neglected tracings of the soul

- that notes are a matter of life and death, as Audre Lorde reminds us, the non-person is she of whom it will be said, "no note taken," while others we might say, are duly noted and dutifully too

- that context is everything—like the question of what I noticed in the worst five minutes of waiting in my life, waiting for 'the news' of a cancer diagnosis—and how I realized more than ever then how I wanted the impossible: for the world to notice that I was in it, while I was living, and to notice, just as significantly, that I'd gone

- that the only definition of "note" worth retaining for our purposes in pursuit of our lecture-art is "any of the basic components of the fragrance of a perfume which give it its character: a component of aroma of food or a flavor, drink, esp. wine." The best notes, the etymology instructs us, are those that combine the musical sense, a sounding, and the hidden comportment of a scent or flavor: a tinge or a tang.

My love of notes and note-taking is essentially sensual, bound together with three memories of feltness from my satchel-clanging school-girl days. There's that combination of care and longing I recall when, too young to read, we'd be sent home with "notes" pinned to the fronts of our plaid uniforms. I'd be out of breath from running or in anticipation of bolting through the door, when a hand without a face would pull me toward it and attach a piece of paper to my person with something written on it. It'd be a message to our mothers about a school assignment or a class trip. The hand was warm, the small, brass safety pin, cold; the paper was white and cotton, the cloth was green and cotton; the press of their finger to my chest was somehow loving or at the very least knowing—it knew that the note would stay affixed in spite of any rough and tumble movements en route with it. I was and wasn't aware of the note, part of it and apart from it; I wanted to know what it contained—to learn to read it—but I also liked the feel of being nothing more than a carrier pigeon and the moment of revelation when, delivering the note in the form of myself to my mother, she would hold it to a light, unfold and decipher it.

There were afternoons, never mornings, when a teacher would announce the occasion of a "film strip." Then we might settle in for a good dose of boredom since "film strips" always also bore the label, "educational." The "film," more like a series of slides that were lent the feeling of cinema by an accompanying soundtrack, would be fed into a contraption by one set of hands, while another set of hands dimmed the lights to nearly total darkness. The metal apparatus gave off pulses of warmth from its motor and the whole affair was accompanied by a fuzzy sounding beep that signaled to the operator (also known as the teacher) to advance the "film." I experienced, if you can believe me, the beep as a *dot*, or point or note, sometimes red, and sometimes black. The voices, on the accompanying cassette tape or record player, often crackled and sometimes gurgled as though suspended in some underwater place—they were never crystal clear, and the dot (I mean beep) would both wake me up and bid me sleep as it slid, Doppler-like, elongating, then contracting, its tone, always out of sync with the image which sometimes would get stuck between frames. It would feel to me then that the room had become layered with a kind of ectoplasmic cookie dough that, hovering around us, urged into being the most surrealistic naps.

Each memory of a note-filled feltness had to do with noticing, which had to do with missing—missing what we'd been told to pay attention to. I don't remember a single piece of information from a slide reel, but I was forever impressed by its intervallic "dot." So, too, with the educator's instrument called "a pointer." I'm not sure what it pointed at, what it aimed for me to see, but I do recall a feeling of experiencing it as a false finger, with a bendy rubber tip. I remember fastening on the way that it softened when it pressed into a blackboard, and smeared the chalk.

•

"A passage of innocent attentions may prove a Paradise indeed."

—Donald Revell, *The Art of Attention: A Poet's Eye*

SECTION THREE: BUTTRESS

By now it must be clear that every era has to reinvent the idea of the note for itself.

Sitting with my poetry-writing students in a garden courtyard one recent fall, I began to realize how all the language I'd been using for the forms of noticing I was interested in asking them to explore bore an uncanny relationship to the juridical. Without intending to, I found myself relying, in our discussions of poetic practice, on a lexicon of witness; summons; and arrest. I had proposed at the outset my own desire for the class: that it could become a community of people present to each other's truths and trials, the creation of beauty, and the tapping of the unsaid. In the first case—"witnessing"—I tried to devise an experiment aimed at loosening a tendency that often besets the inexperienced poet: the temptation to confuse poetry with meaningless abstraction, having nothing to do with the real with which the young writer daily struggles, pitched neither to a recognizable interior, nor exterior, world.

As an exercise, I asked them to begin to pay attention to what they were obsessed with; then to follow this with a record of what they wished they were able to think about instead.

In the succeeding week, I asked them to take a different kind of note based on what they were noticing in the world outside themselves; then an account of what they might do to train their attention to continue to observe it.

By the week after this, we were ready for a more sophisticated relay whose layering might begin to situate them not only squarely in the space of the poem, but in their world. I recommended that we retire to our building's courtyard—a walled in garden, a paradise, a lyceum?—unknown to most people who strolled the building's halls. A professor of Italian had planted many of the shrubs and plants that lined its square, but her garden seemed pre-dated by another person's marvelous version of a mini-arboretum in which small cedars shared a space with a robust and knobby Japanese maple. If you teach a class in the room that looks out onto this courtyard, all you have to do is ask the students to train their attention on the maple and ask what it instructs. Together, you cannot just feel, but literally witness, its changing form with the turn of weeks that defines the semester, ode to a shared inhabitance of time. The thing about the plantings in this little-known outdoor lounge is that even in winter, one shrub holds forth with bright red berries alongside the occasional off-season daisy. Now I asked the students to give themselves over to a tri-partite task at 15 minute intervals: first, simply to "witness," and record what they see, based on whatever literal vantage they might choose; second to allow the observation to take them to an interior place—be it a memory, a dream, an associative thought, or a vital word or phrase; third, to return to the ostensibly "outer" world of the courtyard once more, and record again "what they see." To notice if they find themselves wanting to return to the original spot from which they gazed and look again, or to go to a new place in the garden and write of it, either way, compelled by the relay of outside-in and inside-out. The harder next step was, in the ensuing week, to make a poem born of these notes. For one poet, that yielded the astonishing lines: "a maroon so deep/it resembles a hole/one might fear to/ fall into/so instead/it takes its time to spil/l into/what is left/ of the shade produced/from chlorophyll, a/green so dark one/ might question/what is the line/between/green and black.// linear, straight like a/stick I might throw for you,/or the leash that/guided me down/further into that night,/and I cannot recognize/even the thumping/in my chest."

We spend a lot of time talking about presence in this class—how to be present and how to feel present; the extent to which the world is waiting for us to be present to it, waiting for us to be in it, to find ourselves in it and sing back to its calibrations. One thing I have discovered in my own life as a writer is that certain realities will wait for me to notice them, undyingly, in spite of years and years of thumb-twiddling ignorance and stupidity; others will not, and are bound to be forever lost to me (one day the leaves are tinged in red, the next day, disappeared, I missed them, and they won't, in all their particularity, hold out for me, or return). When I want to drive home the power of witnessing in poetry, I usually turn to the example of Anna Akhmatova, whose poem, "Requiem" shows witnessing to be a matter of life and death. There she famously describes how "during the frightening years of the Yezhov terror" she stood waiting in prison queues in Leningrad for months on end, hoping to get a glimpse of her son, when a woman who somehow recognized her to be a poet, without exactly recognizing who she was, approached her. This woman asks her bluntly whether the scene they are experiencing can be described. Akhmatova replies that, yes, it can, and yes, she will describe it.

Here's what was astonishing to me: that before we could even begin to experience witnessing as a kind of ethical noting, or observational truth-telling, we had to work through my students' sense that "to witness" meant passively to look: it turns out they attach the word to "bystander," and think of witnessing as something accidental, un-willed, uninvolved, even complacent. For them, witnessing is affiliated with the sublimely untouched. At first, in other words, they couldn't consider it as an imperative either to the life of a poet or to life on earth. In that same courtyard meeting, or shortly thereafter, I found myself asking if they'd ever felt summoned, what was summoning them? Did they feel called, and how could this bring them closer to whatever might urge itself onto the page? They admitted to being mainly summoned by their cellphones, so where could they locate the errand that might bring them to their art? To answer what is calling me and why, today, now? It was only when we arrived at "arrest" in our discussions that I realized how a language more relative to law and its enforcements was insinuating itself into the class.

We were talking à la Robert Hass and David Antin about poetic images, those images that hold us fast, and those that, conversely, invite us in, narratively; those that resist our interpretive mechanisms; those that still the object, that are, themselves, objects on a page, and that subsequently still their subject—us. I was trying to ask what is gained by our being arrested by a poem and whether any of them had ever been arrested by such when one student interpreted the question literally and recounted the story of his childhood arrest. We can be held, or taken in, for questioning; we can be stopped inside our motions, immobilized and stilled, politically; and, we can be held, or taken in, stopped in our tracks, stirred inside a silence, aesthetically. What is the bridge between the politics of our daily lives and of our art?

Each era reinvents the idea of the note for itself: if ours is the era of witness-summons-arrest, it must have to do with what we are witnessing but not acting on, and how my immigrant neighbors are being arrested without the summons as a kind of chance. What this might mean for the lecture, or the essay, is that the public nature of its address is under threat, that the well around which we might otherwise gather and commune is literally laced with poison. It is rather difficult if not impossible to notice in a world where we are perpetually surveyed.

I used to think it was important, and I still do, to investigate words more commonly associated with noting—like document, observe, study, attend—to see what they might yield if we look at them askew. Now, more than ever, I believe we must.

Document, observe, study, attend—each represents an attitude of mind that is essential to the cultivation of a non-fictive sensibility; and, just as one or the other might take front seat inside a lecture, each is sure to take up residence more or less centrally in each writer's aesthetic of nonfiction prose.

Immigrant Subjectivity and Documentary Discourse: that was the name of a course I taught twenty years ago on the ways that immigrants create documentary art as acts of resistance to their being documented by the state. "Improper Documents": that's a phrase I used to like to use when I wanted to argue for the importance of documents that resist our filing systems, or undo our attempts to contain the realities they bare. More recently, on the eve of the 2020 election, I feel the urgency of a return to documentary as strict record keeping, and I'm almost hopeful that such a thing is possible—I mean the keeping of an archive, like the one a young journalist compiled soon after Trump was elected to the White House. Matt Kizer's WTFJHT (whatthefuckjusthappenedtoday), subtitled, "today's essential guide to the daily shock and awe in national politics" actively remembers for us in the age of forgetting. In this era when each new offense obliterates our memory of the one that preceded it, WTFJHT supplies a daily, indispensible chronicle of articles, drawn from the most reliable sources, of the Administration's scarcely believable acts. The more matter-of-fact, the more dispassionate, even, the archive, the more likely disbelief will be replaced by recognition. Humor also plays about the edges of Matt Kizer's record—a recording of history that one has to hope will never be erased—but only insofar as the record keeper allows the Administration's words to speak *for themselves* in all their insane, and ridiculous glory. Each day is identified by a kind of vital word or phrase that made headlines that day, issued most often from the mouth of the Administration. On December 11, 2019, the day on which I write, that word is "Scum." Last year's word-phrase on this day was "This Wall Thing"; and the year before, in and around the same day, it was "This Pile of Garbage."

Each writer has to determine for himself how she will foreground or define the figures in our lists: document, observe, study, attend.

Observation interests me, as I have said, to the extent that I need to learn what I can observe in an age of being simultaneously influenced and surveyed.

In twenty-first century America, there is so much that holds or demands our attention without requiring our attention or altering our attention. Attention, I believe, needn't be understood as a defensive posture, the primitive reflex that we mount in response to a threat—*Attenzione! Achtung! Watch out!*, but could re-find its roots in an attitude of tending, caring, watering, nurturing.

As for study, it's what leaves me yearning, in this lecture, for a revolutionized syllabus, the score that sets the pace for our arrival together at an island of difference, open to lingering, and motivated by a collective desire to understand.

·

"At this moment as so often happens in London, there was a complete lull and suspension of traffic. Nothing came down the street; nobody passed. A single leaf detached itself from the plane tree at the end of the street, and in that pause and suspension fell. Somehow it was like a signal falling, a signal pointing to a force in things which one had overlooked."

—Virginia Woolf, *A Room of One's Own*

SECTION FOUR: WING

A company called Field Notes produces a 48-page memo book that invites you to record "crop predictions, small schematics, hate mail, gambling debts, tall orders, escape routes, shady transactions, loose promises, and last will/testament." The size of a pocket book, this product that boasts "durable materials/made in the USA" is only equaled in my mind to the NAP LOG created by "mincingmockingbird," designed in Los Angeles, manufactured in China. I don't know where the materials come from, but the Chinese manufacturer has convincingly reproduced the impression of a softly worn antiquarian book-of-yore in green matte, held together with a light gold spine lightly embossed with barely visible shapes and figures that also give the impression of having been worn slightly down. I guess you could say this notebook seems charmingly "distressed." Do such consumer products anticipate, or actively produce, my interest in the note(book)? If they conflate the seriousness of our subject with the whimsy of a hobbyist, no matter. The lecturer, like the essayist, is nothing if not an amateur.

When was the last time you allowed someone to read to you? When the last time you longed for this? To read you to sleep or to read you awake? The lecture hovers between the two, and its most heightened response—which is also its favorite temporality—is the nap. The lecture's most de-familiarizing power might be its invitation to us to sleep in some place other than our beds, and in this it conjures our earliest memories of being read to, as though we cannot find that place in our adulthood beds, but must be jettisoned to a space unbecoming us wherein some kind guide, gathered for a purpose, unselfish, invites us over a threshold and bids us rest.

We begin in darkness and return to darkness and in between are granted a modicum of light, and thus the lecture shines a light into the light, or better, allows us, for a spell, the growth agent that only wakens in the dark. Darkness stimulates!

No fog, no lecture: in attending a lecture, I am hopeful to exchange one fog for another, sometimes a brighter fog, other times one navigated with more confidence, one that distracts me from my own fog by introducing a more enticing one, a fog to layer atop my own, thence to sleep. But fog is not what we need you say; we need water untrammelled by pollutants, and air, too, clear as bells. My point is just that: at the lecture I encounter a fog that makes the ship that is my body clearer in its outline than ever before, and I get there by way of the LULL.

There was a lull in the lecture, the ripe pause: you missed everything else, even "stopped listening," but you needed the sound of the voice in order to continue to pursue the thing the lecture gave to you. The juncture in a lecture when I become fixated on my notes requires the voice of the lecturer on-go-ingly. In a Stephen Jay Gould Tanner lecture, I pause on the detail of how a tiny bone that had served as the gill-support in fishes came in time to take up residence in the mammalian inner ear. I missed whatever the rest of the lecture was about, but I need his voice to stay here. The room absent the voice would be like draining the room of water and expecting you to continue to swim. Once under, it'd be like subtracting the fog-horn or sonar that enables us to remain submerged.

What is a nap in this context but a non-affirming nod, a type of note?

I'm not listening, and I'm not not listening. I'm noting, which is not the same as circling a pen round and round the dot that perforates the spiral of a ringed notebook, boring down, boring in, possibly bored. Or so I used to think until I read cartoonist Lynda Barry's *Syllabus*, the book based on her course called "Unthinkable Mind." *Start with a dot, spiral a line around it and keep going*, Barry instructs her students: "it's an exercise in both relaxation and concentration," she explains, and "your task is to get the lines as close together as possible without letting them touch. If they touch, you get electrocuted." Barry's directions encourage a kind of self-hypnosis that enables one part of the mind to wake while the other simultaneously sleeps. Ergo: make spirals all you want during the lecture. This does not mean you are not noting; maybe you've discovered the native power of drawing labyrinths without benefit of instruction and this is your doorway to the place where you become someone other than yourself, for haven't you come to the lecture in the first place hoping to be released temporarily from whatever you are perpetually recovering from?

Your eyes close and a book opens to the page where you last left off, on the beach, or on the train, forgetfully, the book you forgot having lent and never saw again, the book that was stolen and the one that fell right through the cracks in a grate, the book they never finished reading to you because the violence interrupted. The nap is the breeze that reopens those pages and asks you to reach inside.

To grant sleep to someone is "the very act of benevolence" for it gives the sleeper "the power to be utterly confident." This is one of Barthes' more beautifully translatable recordings in the collection of his lecture notes, *The Neutral*.

Where is the lecturer who wishes for us to nap, uncertain what we will note, averse to the dictator's dictation?

Let the lecture resume on a new note tomorrow.

·

IV.

BRIEF ENCOUNTERS

WITH SOME

LECTURING MODES

EXCURSION;
COMPRESSION;
ADAPTATION AND
REINVENTION

"And, of course, I am afraid—you can hear it in my voice—because the transformation of silence into language and action is an act of self-revelation and that always seems fraught with danger."

—Audre Lorde, "The Transformation of Silence
into Language and Action"

I'm convinced that I learned how to read and I learned how to write by listening to the Americanist scholar Martin Pops lecture. When my mentor, the great essayist, Marty Pops gave this lecture on Henry James' *The Aspern Papers* at SUNY/Buffalo in 1985, he hadn't lineated it, though I'm certain he did *compose* it in the way a musician creates a score. He was the age I am now when he wrote this lecture-as-incantation, and I am the age he was then listening to it as though hearing it for the first time and with the fullest, most startling force of its import, of what it not only addresses or invokes but intones. I'm literally listening to the lecture again because I have a cassette recording of it. It was I who had suggested the tape recording when Marty was otherwise to miss his class on account of minor surgery. "I'll bring my recorder to your house," I said. "You can record your lecture in your own time and then I'll bring it to the class so we can listen to it. It appears you're not too ill to lecture, right? It'll be fun."

Listen to the first two minutes of Marty's 90-minute lecture, knowing that it is, in its entirety, rendered like this:

In any case . . .
Pain
arrogates consciousness to itself
as Rabelais argues
in his great book
that the king of all men
to whom even earthly kings
bow down
is *venter*,
the body,
hunger,
a deeply materialist explanation of human events,
that life in the hospital
or in Rabelais,
(though Rabelais is endlessly more exuberant)
is life in the lower body,
(though Rabelais himself allows for the Abbey of Theleme
at the end of his book *Gargantua* a realm of higher
consciousness)
. . . in any case
he is fundamentally concerned
as life in the hospital is fundamentally concerned
with such things as
the consistency of bowel and the quantity of urine,

the blood the bowel the body and the baby talk,
the sacred mystery of your body here revealed,
the private text of your body here inscribed,
it's as if these were newspaper headlines
perhaps you are the victim of vandals
and graffiti.

Near the end of his life,
Henry James, in medical crisis,
it's one of the most touching episodes in James' life,
"sobbed and panted and held my hand"
said his nephew, one of William James' sons,
but that, of course, is not the James we know,
and love,
and it is the James we can hardly imagine,
James reduced to blood, bowel, the body, and baby talk.
No.
The Jamesian protagonist, as we have observed,
is out to "see, to see all she can,"
"to live, live all he can,"
the passionate pilgrim of a higher consciousness,
one who, like John Marcher in the *Beast in the Jungle*,
awaits the event,
the distinguished thing,
(James called "a distinguished thing" the onset as he thought
    it of his own death)
awaits the unique experience.

Mrs. Prest says in *The Aspern Papers*, "One would think you
    expected to find in those papers, the riddle of the uni-
    verse,"
these papers
which elsewhere are called "sacred relics,"
with
whatever
admitted irony,
and, which are characterized as possessing esoteric knowl-
    edge
again,
with
whatever
admitted irony.
These are, in any case, high stakes,
and stakes away from the lower body.
Or so they seem.

I re-visit Marty's lecture and continue to learn from it 25
years after the fact, understanding just a little bit more than
I had at 25 years of age. These were the utterances not of
an emergent but a fully formed voice, which doesn't mean
that the lecture wasn't full of gaps and hesitations. It is hard to
know, listening back on it, how the unformed blob that I was
heard it, or what part of it I was able to then take in. Marty's
lecture was not really preachy, though it was pronounced in
sacral tones; it preserved the bass-y concatenations of a chant

underscored by the textures of a Brooklyn Jewish accent (the sound of one kind of leather—a baseball's, hitting another kind of leather—the glove). It's a genre that may have gone out of fashion, if it ever existed at all.

It is a parsing of knowledge riddled with enjambment.

It's thinking as a form of breathing.

Though it sounds authoritative, it is all about submission, since it asks a student to witness as a reader submits himself to a book; to listen to the sounds of an idea played upon the improvisatory instrument that is the teacher's voice.

"Arrogate" was a new word for me even at middle-age. "Pain arrogates consciousness to itself"; pain claims consciousness for itself, leaving no room for anything but itself.

(Would you believe me if I told you that I once wrote a 100-page essay based on Marty Pops' lecture—it was based on a book that I stole from his office, a book that he, himself, had written, and that I brought back to him as a parting gift in the last weeks of his life.)

I think what I've been driving at all along is a poetics of the lecture. So let's come back to silence and restraint (neither of which I'm good at), and to poets.

The University of Pennsylvania features something on their website called the 60 Second Lecture. It's a PR ploy to allow prospective students a taste of the kind of thinking that an education at the university affords. The tantalizing minimalist constraint, though, is lost on many of the faculty who feature there—no one really uses the directive to test the form's liberating finitude. Instead, in true academic fashion, each tries to squash as much information as possible into their slot as if in a sort of speed-dating mode until the one minute charge morphs into two, three, and four minutes. In fact, in some cases the constraint seems to have made mad scientist-type figures even more crazed as they rush and sputter to a finish line, unable to pack it all in. Except in the case of experimental poet Charles Bernstein. Rather than use the one-minute lecture to present his subject, he exploits it in order to perform his subject. He occupies time and discovers the amplitude of one minute of utterance or one minute of life. He does this by subverting the positivism of the lecture mode via a series of negations; by fashioning a list poem (that poetic envelope of bounded boundlessness); and by, in the end, literally timing himself without taming himself. He makes the constraint his instructive subject, and, by mapping it onto a matrix of poetic practice, infuses it with JOY. This is this lecture's element of best-of-all: Bernstein uses the lecture mode, à la Roland Barthes, to restore *saveur* to *savoir*, to bring a savoring into contact with a knowing: or in Roland Barthes' words, in his own 1977 lecture to the Collège de France, he makes "knowledge festive."

Here's what Bernstein's lecture sounds like if I take the liberty of lineating it, inserting ellipses both to replicate the power of its pauses and to visualize its sonic teetering between poetry and prose, solid space and enveloping void:

"My lecture is called 'What Makes a Poem and Poem.'

I'm gonna set my timer . . .
It's not . . . rhyming words at the end of a line.
It's not . . . form.
It's not . . . structure.
It's not . . . loneliness.
It's not . . . location.
It's not . . . the sky.
It's not . . . love.
It's not . . . the color.
It's not . . . the feeling.
It's not . . . the meter.
It's not . . . the place.
It's not . . . the intention.
It's not . . . the desire.
It's not . . . the weather.
It's not . . . the hope.
It's not . . . the subject matter.
It's not . . . the death.
It's not . . . the birth.
It's not . . . the trees.
It's not . . . the words.
It's not . . . the thing between the words.
It's not . . . the meter.
It's not . . . the meter

(here the timer on his watch goes off, which he pauses to listen to for several long seconds).

It's the timing."

You will remember John Cage's 1949 and 1950 "Lecture on Something" and "Lecture on Nothing," in which Cage made use of methods similar to those he used as a composer. Fragmented and collaged, Cage's lectures come equipped with answers he would give to the first six questions in Q and A no matter what those questions were. They are:

That is a very good question. I should not want to spoil it with an answer.

My head wants to ache.

Had you heard Marya Freund last April in Palermo singing Arnold Schoenberg's *Pierrot Lunaire*, I doubt whether you would ask that question.

According to the Farmers' Almanack this is False Spring.

Please repeat the question . . . And again . . . and again . . .

I have no more answers.

At least once in a semester, I find, it always pays to visit this particularly stirring moment in John Cage's "Lecture on Nothing" and play it for one's students:

More and more, I have the feeling that we are getting nowhere. Slowly as the talk goes on, we are getting nowhere. And that is a pleasure. It is not irritating to be where one is. It is only irritating to think one would like to be somewhere else. Here we are now. A little bit after the middle of the fourth large part of this talk. More and more, we have the feeling that I am getting nowhere. Slowly, as the talk goes on, slowly, we have the feeling we are getting nowhere. That is a pleasure which will continue. If we are irritated, it is not a pleasure. Nothing is not a pleasure if one is irritated. But suddenly, it is a pleasure. And then more and more it is not irritating. And then more and more, and slowly. Originally, we were nowhere. And now again we are having the pleasure of being slowly nowhere. If anybody is sleepy, let him go, to sleep.

The lecture is this allowance: it says, yes, it is ok to pause, to be lulled, not exactly la-la bye bye, or soporifically into swoon or oblivion, but into a realm of heightened thinking-feeling, blanketing perhaps, cradling us, even, but not coddling, though there be pleats and folds of ideas tucked inside ideas. Such hum, loll, prattle, mutter as this can augur a calm before a storm, a brewing, though it may also introduce nothing more than a pleasing quiescence unopposed to action, more, its cultivated ground.

What *is* a lecture, you might ask now, after all is said and done, have I adequately answered the question? In a series of strange coincidences, I find three leading philosophical lights—Simone Weil, Michel Foucault, and Roland Barthes—each in their way comparing the lecture to an OBJECT. In her thoughts on the type of true attention required by study—"Reflections on the Right Use of School Studies with a View to the Love of God"— Simone Weil likens knowledge to an object that "penetrates" us.

But I'd prefer an image of being brushed, and in that encounter, sounded or stirred. I don't go to a lecture to be vanquished—daily life is already quite accomplished in demolishing me; nor do I care for the experience of being pierced. I think, rather, I know, that the lecture can make possible a co-mingling—better than an ASMR tingling—that might leave me breathless, but at its best helps me remember *that* I breathe.

Foucault, curiously, likens the lecture to the fashioning of "a shoe," as he puts it, "no more no less." "I design an object," he tells his interviewer, "I try to make it as well as possible. I make a lot of trouble for myself (not always, perhaps, but often), I bring the object to the desk, I show it and then I leave it up to the audience to do with it what they want. I consider myself more like an artisan doing a certain piece of work and offering it for consumption than a master making his slaves work." As a person who descends from artisans—metallurgists, hatters (note my surname), gardeners, weavers, embroiderers, confectioners, and as I have already described, shoemakers, I hesitate to use "artisanal" metaphorically, and I dare not underestimate, as I believe Foucault does, what it takes to make a shoe. I know my grandfather mastered far more many materials than I in the shoes that he crafted, and that he called upon far more many types of skill and intuition in making shoes than what it takes to scratch these words onto a pad in writing or scratch the dandruff off my brow in lecturing.

Barthes thinks of his lecture as an object but adds a psychological twist to the mix, when, in his Lecture before the

Collège de France that I have plumbed quite happily more than once in this lecture, he likens "the speaking and the listening that will be interwoven here to . . . the comings and goings of a child playing beside his mother, leaving her, returning to bring her a pebble, a piece of string, and thereby tracing around a calm center a whole locus of play within which the pebble, the string come to matter less than the enthusiastic giving of them." While we might grant him the dislodgement of the objects themselves which come to matter less than the act of play made possible by them, or the calm center around which they coalesce, it's still curious to me that pebbles, strings, and mothers should be brought to bear on lecturing; moreover, *as we will all remember,* one really cannot as a twentieth century Frenchman invoke either string or *mamma* without echoing Freud's famous mother and famous string in his description of the game called "fort-da" / "here-gone": it's the disappearing act a baby carries out in the nursery with his spool, hiding it from himself, then making it appear again, so as to master the defining and definitive, eventual and inevitable absence of his mother. In Barthes' metaphor, the mother is not absent but re-animated in you and me, his audience; the unifying components of fort-da have disintegrated into fragments, now re-deposited into his mother's lap. I'm not sure what to make of this—that the utopian lecture hall might have reparation at its heart—and performance on a potty. (I know that all of my exhibitionistic pleasures date back to the initial applause—I recall it well—that followed my ascension and successful conquest of that kiddy-throne, though I hadn't till now considered that toilet training might also function as fort-da when we make the poop appear and then, fast as a flash, flush it down.) Child-mind might need to be pre-eminent when we climb onto the lecturing stage because we're never not invulnerable, no matter how high the podium might make us seem, and we'll get nowhere if we don't humble ourselves before the knowledge we also claim to master.

In any case, by now it should be clear: I do not think of the lecture as an object, but as a type of voicing and of song whose intention is not for you to consume it, judge it, survey it, accept it or reject it (what objects generally require) but *to move with it* to places un-fore-told in oneself and in the world.

What IS a lecture? It lives on the stage and not on this page; it is essentially improvisatory. (If Whitman may repeat himself, mightn't I?) Unlike written prose, the lecture, Erving Goffman reminds us, can interrupt itself and with "the help of an audible change in voice, interject something that is flagrantly irrelevant"; it can call upon "colloquialisms and irreverences" that the lecturer "is likely to censor in the printed text." When lecturing, she can "exaggerate, be dogmatic, say things that obviously aren't quite fully true, and omit documentation." Though a person might repeat a lecture for different audiences, lectures must convey "a first and only illusion," and of course their degree of freshness also depends largely on the feel the audience itself conveys, hopefully not, in its unresponsiveness, "freezing [the lecturer] to his script."

There is much more at stake in the voice and presence that

the lecture requires than the written words absent their author that define a book: think of Plotinus who refused to commit his lectures to writing and preferred instead the perpetual alterations they underwent by his auditors' questions. There is much more at stake in the bodily inhabitance, the more or less license you grant me of this voice. The Diné writer Rhiannon Sorrell, of the Kinłichíí'nii (Red House People) and Ta'neezahnii (Tangle People) clans, said it best: "The tyranny of silence threatens to consume us every day. Perhaps we keep it at bay through writing, through the notebook, but we know that we have to exorcise the aphonic demon that tolerates our writing but not our voice." The lecture is courageous in ways that writing is not, especially if we consider the new brands of mean-spiritedness that characterize our day. Hannah Arendt addressed the matter stirringly five decades ago in ways that we can still apply today: "Without a politically guaranteed public realm," she said, "freedom lacks the worldly space to make its appearance . . . Courage . . . is demanded of us . . . even to leave the protective security of our four walls and enter the public realm, not because of particular dangers which may or may not lie in wait for us, but because we have arrived in a realm *where the concern for life has lost its validity*" (italics mine). Retreat into the page is easy compared with a member of congress confronting her angry constituents on why she voted for impeachment—it's astonishing to listen to the vitriol they hurl at her, the misogyny they fling her way, the stomping of their voices heavy as feet. Maybe we should replace all lectures with the articulateness, itself a form of heroism, of Fiona Hill.

The lecture—I wish you could have been there!—resists covers, a slipknot, and a paper bag. (It's more like stand-up.) It wants to be held, but it may not wish to be kept on a shelf, and especially one that also holds the pottery and knick-knacks. Once cast in the form of a book, it can't afford to trip you up with questions; rather, it will have you pause for flaws, and excite your betrayal for its lack of polish.

Ah! But certain writing—the writing most akin to the lecture—is nothing if not the product of an "imperfect intelligence" (to quote Mario Praz): of course I'm talking about the essay as conceived by practitioners of the form the world over, the essay as the genre that fails to be a genre, that begins with missteps, then allows for a tendency, not of correction (the editorial mode) but of allowance, intent on playing hooky. Both the lecture and the essay know that erring is a kind of errancy, never to be discounted as much as mined. Still, there are significant departures between the two: there are things I can gloss over in a lecture that I can't afford to when a lecture hits the page. This is why I hope that you interlard your notes between these lines, then recreate the whole in the form of confetti; this is why I ask that we, together, first and foremost, recognize that these pages are much like our bodies, fragile as parchment, slivering nearer and nearer to dust each moment, each day.

Because the lecture is all voice, it is never as absolute as its own pronouncements (thank goodness). It can be riddled with untraceable sources and full of mistakes; it might in fact amount to nothing more than a series of all that the lecturer mistook, tokens of a hazy memory, divined through her fingers as they read 'cross the pages of piles and piles of books, enough to make a magician's home inside of. Consider my reference to Woolf, Einstein and Freud in this lecture's opening sentence. Can I do justice to the collapse and the elision therein? Was this an instance of an irresponsible, because unexplained, or just un-pursued apposition? To determine what I meant by bringing those three and the question of war into the same space would require labor, and the lecture is essentially lazy; it is also always short on time. It's not that Woolf wrote of lectures and lecturing while Freud and Einstein discussed the nature of war. Woolf of course also posed and answered this question—why war?—wondering along with them if war could be prevented, and possibly answered it better than those two, though I am not at the moment at liberty to judge (that would require more time), in her book *Three Guineas*. Woolf also, I suspect, understood that a relationship inhered *between* lecturing and war, bolstered as both are by a patriarchal purview.

But my casting of Woolf as anti-lecture is also not entirely accurate. She seems to have hated lecturing—"I can't bear lecturing; it takes ages; and I do it vilely," she wrote as she prepared the lecture that would serve as the basis for *A Room of One's Own*. She suffered—but who doesn't?—alienation from her audience-in-public, perhaps, then, not quite in touch with or willing to muster the particular type of courage we find in the public servant I cited earlier and in Fiona Hill. But she wasn't opposed to all lecturing, absolutely and for all time. In *Three Guineas* she qualifies her assertion for those who would mistake her: "No one," she writes, "would maintain that all lecturers and all lectures are 'vain and vicious,'" quoting herself, and she goes on to explain that the particular lecture she considers obsolete and worthy of abolition are those delivered to "sons and daughters of educated men" on the subject of English literature, reducing that vast art to an "examination subject" and rendering students "mentally docile" in the process.

What Woolf did not do, and what I wish she could talk to us about from the great beyond, was to create a form of lecturing that could adequate the radical inventiveness of her fiction.

There is so much that lies unrevealed in the lecture in general, and in this lecture in particular. Though a reader might assume that my sources are in evidence as citations, my thinking, just like yours, actually derives from a mostly invisible "uncommon archive"—my pet phrase—or what Barthes would call a plurality of desires and reservoir of perversions that lay at the heart of any creation and must be allowed free play. As textured as our notes and as untranslatable, they include, for me, my mother's agoraphobia and the time bomb that was my father; the boom of my father's voice that knocked out each rib that held a breath in place, and sometimes his hand; the scent of a gardener's gardenias in my mother's hair (the gardener was my father); the sound that broke the dinner plates in the same moment it killed the little girl next door when a bullet aimed at her father struck her down instead; the daily search for the antidote; my first encounter with the word "crepuscular," my sense there was something to be learned of "crenellations"; getting lost in a department store when I was seven and in a snow bank when I was eight; the particular gracefulness of a flying squirrel who glided across branches in a future sleep; the tendency to curve, coil, spring and screw in spite of all the world's attempts to straighten, stiffen and stuff.

I do believe that the type of lecture I've been asking you to fantasize with me, where benevolence reigns and a peaceable kingdom is sought after, is traceable to my all-too-intimate, direct experiences and perpetual witnessing of, violence, not only on the working class streets where I grew up, but in the place that should have been reserved for nurturance and inclusion, the classroom. In the elementary school rooms of Catholicism that shaped me, corporal punishment reigned supreme, and even the teachers were not spared (a founding trauma of my childhood was the sting and terror of this sight: my witnessing a Mother Superior slap one of my favorite teachers across the face). The lecture—but who could have told this without having begun to think about rather than simply recite the lecture in the first place—takes as its origin violence and war. And now I am happy to give you what I promised early on but could not myself have anticipated: my origin of the podium was a fanciful invention, but this one of the "rostrum" is true.

The rostrum, a platform stand for public speakers in the

Forum of Ancient Rome, is Latin for "beak," but it doesn't have the thrush in mind, a gentle chirping, soft tufts of feathers, or the hungry, open mouths of baby chicks. It's a reference to a beak-like projection on battleships that would be used to ram the vessel of an enemy. Such "rostrum" would be arrayed upon the stage to indicate triumph in the spoils of war, in this way, bestowing martial authority—here, one and the same—on the speaker. The literal meaning of "rostrum" derives from the verb form "rodere," "to scrape, scratch, or gnaw." Isn't that what you think of when you hear the verb "lecture"? Once the word is extended to embrace any sense of a platform for public speaking, it offers an origin, now invisible, of a lecture hall as a place where I sport my plunder, the podium, as the symbol that directs you to follow the command of my voice. The rostrum is a war trophy, and the speaker the embodiment of vanquishing force.

In preparing this lecture, I brought my dog-eared copy of Toni Morrison's lectures, *Playing in the Dark*, back onto my desk. And I listened to three lectures delivered at three different junctures in her illustrious career: one in 1991, An Address to the Second Chicago Humanities Festival; one on "Goodness: Altruism and the Literary Imagination" delivered to the Harvard Divinity School in 2012; and her Nobel Prize acceptance speech. I listened to these lectures in my car en route to my workplace at a university, and it's not a listening space I recommend. In my own state of Rhode Island, there are new ways that fellow drivers have of cutting you off without a signal, as if you are not there and they are threatening, if you announce yourself, to kill you, they come so close, within a hair's breadth of your fender or your door. In the all-caps capitalist world in which I live, I drive a car beset with sensors that translate reality into a barrage of incoming threats that keeps me jumpy and vigilant. This same era grants me endless interruptive mechanisms as I seat myself before the wheel intent on focus: at any moment, when I least expect it, Toni Morrison's voice or the profusion of forsythia that signal Spring might be cut through by the sudden incursion of blarings from my phone that I'm not even aware of having stowed there—The Beach Boys' insipid "Wouldn't It Be Nice" (The Beach Boys?); a voice in an endless loop saying "quid pro quo"; the kerplunk of an incoming text; the scree of an incoming call; the ping, at top volume, that tells me my drug supply is ready for pick up at the local pharmacy. It is difficult if not impossible to observe in a world where we are constantly surveyed. In the earliest lecture of Morrison's that I tried to listen to, she speaks of the dire consequences of an unschooled life; of "how much American education costs if you go, and how much it costs, if you don't." She wishes for a nation state of intelligent, curious, educated people. And she describes the then current student body in words I can also apply thirty years later in manifold ways to my own: she calls them "grief stricken and terrified." Is this not enough of a reason to re-design our plans for the lecture? To mount a movement against our collective ban on listening? To re-determine how the lecture can meet us ear to ear, and eye to eye?

Carl Bode opines in his book on the lyceum that "the mass media of radio, motion pictures, and television [and now we could add the Internet] have triumphed unconditionally over the lecture." I don't agree. Rather than render the lecture obsolete, rather than negate or displace the lecture, they have each in their way called for a newly vital lecture mode. We just haven't known how to heed their call and reinvent. We haven't cared to create a lecture that could adequate the essay once more. But which essay would that be? An essay rendered in an earlier age whose form has not yet been exhausted, or a twenty-first century essay: a lecture that could "work against information machines toward the creation of a new *becoming art*, to deliver us from our informational automatisms and our communicational stupidities." (I'm quoting John Rajchman here on Gilles Deleuze.)

In the recurring lecture nightmare, the students aren't paying attention, but this misses the point of the lecture as I want to dream it while we're still awake. Because the lecture, if it's doing its job, must suspend one form of attention in order to allow another form to wake.

"Lectures for me are bad dreams," says Mary Ruefle. "A professor's sole activity [is] to dream his research aloud," says Roland Barthes.

Perhaps at the end we must conclude that I have not lectured but have dreamed—yes, I've been dreaming up here—which doesn't mean that this lecture never took place, but that the place in which it occurred is not one accessible without an alteration of sense and sensibility. It is available only so long as we long, so long as we listen, and note. Yes, I've been dreaming up here, which is to say, hoping to conjure lost souls, lost loves, lost arts, and lost teachers.

We're 121 pages in, and I've not yet asked the most important question: when will we build the rooms to meet the form of our inquiry or of art rather than slot every talk, panel and reading into the same rank and file? How can nonfiction's lost performative call us to listen in terms of a different arrangement? What keeps us holding fast to forms we barely know the origin or import of? The assumptions that undergird them, the effects they serve, the modes of knowing and desiring that they keep in place?

Now I want a meeting place fashioned of differently angled and differently scaled inclined planes. Instead of sitting at long tables, each person lies on her back looking up. Each speaks without facing the other as at a campsite at nightfall, our documents in common: one star-stud or a spiel of constellations. Some are silent, while others carouse and carry on. Everyone murmurs on the verge of sleep.

But this is for another lecture.

•

ACKNOWLEDGMENTS

I would like to thank Eric LeMay, Dinty Moore, Dave Wanczyk, and Sarah Minor whose invitation to deliver a reading and a "lecture" at Ohio University's Spring 2017 Literary Festival provided the opportunity for my bringing some of these formulations to the stage (and to the page); Philip Graham who generously sought to publicize the original lecture in a Special Artist Feature of *Ninth Letter*; and, Maria Tumarkin through whose encouragement the initial short-form lecture made its way to this fuller, extended meditation, to Adam Levy, and to Transit Books. I also wish to acknowledge Abby Nigro and Rhiannon Sorrell, parts of whose poems I cite herein as they were conveyed to me in undergraduate and graduate seminars at the University of Rhode Island. I am indebted to the late Georgiana Peacher for introducing me to the unusual multimodal presentations of Mary Brooks Adelsperger. Without the following interlocutors, there is, for me, no lecture: David Antin, *Lemons/A Talk Poem*, University of Texas/Arlington, 1983 (© 1987 High Performance Audio Cassette) / Hannah Arendt, "Freedom and Politics: A Lecture," *Chicago Review*, vol. 14, no. 1 (Spring 1960): 28-46 / James Baldwin, "Who Is the Nigger?" a clip from *Take This Hammer*, KQED/National Education Television, 1963 / Lynda Barry, *Syllabus: Notes from an Accidental Professor*, (Drawn and Quarterly/Farrar, Straus and

Giroux, 2014) / Roland Barthes, "Lecture In Inauguration of the Chair of Literary Semiology, Collège de France, January 7, 1977," *October*, vol. 8, Spring 1979: 3-16 / Roland Barthes, *The Neutral, Lecture Course at the Collège de France (1977-78)*, (NY: Columbia University Press, 2005) / Charles Bernstein, "What Makes a Poem a Poem?" The UPenn 60 Second Lecture Series: / Carl Bode, *The American Lyceum: Town Meeting of the Mind* (NY: Oxford UP, 1956) / Louise Bogan, *Journey Around My Room: The Autobiography of Louise Bogan, A Mosaic* by Ruth Limmer (NY: Penguin, 1980) / John Cage, *Silence: Lectures and Writings* (Middletown, CT: Wesleyan University Press, 1961) and "Mushroom Haiku, excerpt from Silence," 1972/69, available on UbuWeb, "Sound," John Cage (1912-1992); / Gilles Deleuze and Claire Parnet, *Gilles Deleuze: From A to Z*, Pierre-Andre Boutang (director), Charles J. Stivale (translator), (Los Angeles: Semiotext(e), 2012) / Alexis DeVeaux, *Warrior Poet: A Biography of Audre Lorde* (NY: WW Norton, 2006) / Stephen Dobyns, "Notes on Free Verse" in *Best Words/Best Order: Essays on Poetry* (NY: Palgrave/Macmillan 2003) / The Einstein-Freud Correspondence (1931-1935), available on-line, public.asu.edu / William Gass, "Emerson and the Essay," in *Habitations of the Word* (NY: Simon and Schuster, 1985) / Erving Goffman, *Forms of Talk* (Philadelphia: University of Pennsylvania Press, 1981) / Susan Gubar, "Introduction" to Virginia Woolf's *A Room of One's Own* (NY: Harcourt, 2005) / Richard Hamblyn, *The Invention of Clouds: How An Amateur Meteorologist Forged the Language of the Skies* (NY: Picador, 2002)

/ Robert Hass, "Image," in *Twentieth Century Pleasures: Prose on Poetry* (Ecco Press, 2000) / Siri Hustvedt, "Inside the Room" in *A Woman Looking at Men Looking at Women* (NY: Simon and Schuster, 2016) / Henry James, *The Bostonians* (NY: The Modern Library, 1956) / Audre Lorde, "The Transformation of Silence into Language and Action" in *Sister Outsider: Essays and Speeches* (Trumansburg, NY: Crossing Press Feminist Series, 2007), originally delivered at the Lesbian Literature Panel of the MLA, December 28, 1977 / Steven Meyer, *Irresistible Dictation: Gertrude Stein and the Correlations of Writing and Science* (California: Stanford UP, 2001) / Toni Morrison, Address to the Second Chicago Humanities Festival, 1991, Word of Mouth Series / Cynthia Ozick, "She: Portrait of the Essay as a Warm Body" in *Quarrel and Quandary: Essays* (NY: Knopf, 2000) / Georges Perec, *An Attempt at Exhausting a Place in Paris* translated by Marc Lowenthal (Wakefield Press, 2010) / John Rajchman, *The Deleuze Connections* (Cambridge, Massachusetts: MIT Press, 2000) / Sir Arthur Quiller-Couch ("Q"), *A Lecture on Lectures* Introductory Volume (London: The Hogarth Press, 1927) / Mary Ruefle, *Madness, Rack, and Honey: Collected Lectures* (Seattle: Wave Books, 2012) / Donald Revell, *The Art of Attention: A Poet's Eye* (Saint Paul, MN: Graywolf Press, 2007) / Jenna Sauers, "Anne Carson Wants Her Writing to Move You," *Jezebel*, March 15, 2013 / John K. Simon, "A Conversation with Michel Foucault," *The Partisan Review*, Spring 1971: 192-201 / Dziga Vertov and Kevin O'Brian, "The Factory of Facts and Other Writings," *October*, vol. 7, Soviet Revolutionary Culture (Winter, 1978): 109-128 / Simone Weil, "Reflections on the Right Use of School Studies with a View to the Love of God" in *Waiting on God* (London: Routledge, 1951) / Virginia Woolf, "Why?" in *The Death of the Moth and Other Essays* (NY: Harcourt, 1970), and *Three Guineas*, Annotated and with an Introduction by Jane Marcus (NY: Harcourt, 2006). The image of Mary Brooks Adelsperger's lecture brochure is courtesy of the Redpath Chautauqua Collection, University of Iowa Libraries, Iowa City, Iowa.

Mary Cappello's six books of literary nonfiction include a detour on awkwardness; a breast-cancer anti-chronicle; a lyric biography; and the mood fantasia, *Life Breaks In*. A former Guggenheim and Berlin Prize Fellow, she is a professor of English and creative writing at the University of Rhode Island. She lives in Providence, Rhode Island, and Lucerne-in-Maine, Maine.

Undelivered Lectures is a narrative nonfiction series featuring book-length essays in slim, handsome editions.

01 Mary Cappello, *Lecture*

Transit Books is a nonprofit publisher of international and American literature, based in Oakland, California. Founded in 2015, Transit Books is committed to the discovery and promotion of enduring works that carry readers across borders and communities. Visit us online to learn more about our forthcoming titles, events, and opportunities to support our mission.

TRANSITBOOKS.ORG